Taschentrainer Englisch

John Stevens

True and False Friends

Stolpersteine im englischen Wortschatz

Hueber Verlag

Taschentrainer Englisch

ist eine Reihe von Übungsbüchern im kleinen Format für schnelles und bequemes Üben für zu Hause und unterwegs. Mit den Taschentrainern werden Grammatik, Wortschatz und Sprachgebrauch in authentischen Situationen wiederholt, gefestigt und vertieft. Die Reihe ist optimal für das Selbststudium geeignet.

3. 2. 1. | Die letzten Ziffern
2013 12 11 10 09 | bezeichnen Zahl und Jahr des Druckes.
Alle Drucke dieser Auflage können, da unverändert, nebeneinander benutzt werden.
1. Auflage

Umschlaggestaltung: Parzhuber und Partner, München
Fotogestaltung Cover: wentzlaff | pfaff | güldenpfennig kommunikation gmbh, München
Coverfoto: © Matton Images/StockByte
Redaktion: Valerio Vial, Hueber Verlag, Ismaning
Zeichnungen: Irmtraud Guhe, München
Layout und Satz: appel media, Oberding
Druck und Bindung: Ludwig Auer GmbH, Donauwörth
Printed in Germany
ISBN 978-3-19-057918-1

Inhalt

Vorwort

Liebe Englischlernende,

die *Taschentrainer Englisch* sind ideal für das schnelle und bequeme Lernen zwischendurch. Das kleine, handliche Format passt in jede Tasche. So können Sie jederzeit, zu Hause und unterwegs, Übungen machen.

Mit dem vorliegenden Taschentrainer lernen Sie, wichtige englische Wörter in häufig auftretenden Alltagssituationen korrekt anzuwenden. Behandelt werden neben *False friends* auch weitere typische Wortverwechslungen und Fehlerquellen – diese finden Sie unter den Bezeichnungen *Confusing friends, True friends* und *Lots of friends.* Der letzte Abschnitt des Taschentrainers *(All friends together)* ist weitgehend als Wiederholung der Teile A.–D. gedacht. Einen Überblick über sämtliche Themenbereiche und deren Schwerpunkte erhalten Sie durch das Inhaltsverzeichnis auf S. 3.

In diesem Taschentrainer finden Sie

- über 100 abwechslungsreiche und unterhaltsame Übungen;
- authentische Situationen und Kontexte aus dem Alltags- und Berufsleben;
- einen übersichtlichen Lösungsteil zur Selbstkontrolle;
- ergänzende Erklärungen über die Bedeutung der geübten Wörter (im Lösungsteil nach dem Symbol ▶).

Der vorliegende Taschentrainer ist als Begleitmaterial für die Kompetenzniveaus A2 bis B2 des Gemeinsamen Europäischen Referenzrahmens konzipiert. Er ist bestens zur Evaluation geeignet, um zu testen, was man gut oder weniger gut beherrscht.

Viel Spaß mit Ihrem Taschentrainer!

Autor und Verlag

A. True friends?

Englisch-deutsche Wortpaare mit ähnlicher Form und ähnlicher Bedeutung – aber nicht immer!

A1 I'll take you. *bringen / bring*

Was passt zusammen? Ordnen Sie zu.

1. I'll take you
2. Can you put
3. Can you bring me
4. I don't want to get you
5. First get the children

a. into difficulties.
b. a cloth, please?
c. to the station.
d. to safety.
e. the children to bed?

Und nun ergänzen Sie *bring* oder *take*.

6. We use _________ for a movement away from the person who is speaking.
7. We use _________ for a movement towards the person who is speaking.

A2 What a day! *bringen / bring*

Ergänzen Sie passende Übersetzungen von „bringen“ aus A1.

What a day! I've been on the go for about 14 hours, non-stop. In the morning they (1.) _________ our new fitted kitchen. Of course there were problems, with pieces missing and pieces that didn't fit, which really (2.) _________ the workmen into difficulties. The whole thing took longer than expected, and two of them had to go off to another job while the third one finished off.
I (3.) _________ him to the bus-stop half an hour ago – not my job I know, but he had such a lot of stuff to carry and had really done a good job, so I took pity on him.
In between making tea for the workmen and picking up the kids from school and trying to prepare the presentation I'm giving in Berlin next week, I had to (4.) _________ Julian to the airport. He's gone to Stockholm for a week, on business. I told him not to forget to (5.) _________ something back for the kids. Yes, the kids. It's 9.15, and I've only just (6.) _________ them to bed.

A3 Are you coming? *kommen / come*

Welcher Ausdruck passt in die Lücke?

1. A group of us are going to the pub. Are you ...
   a. coming with — c. by us
   b. coming — d. with us
2. Excuse me. How do I ... to the station?
   a. come — c. get
   b. arrive — d. reach
3. His temperature is really high. I'm going to ... the doctor.
   a. ask to come — c. let come
   b. get to come — d. send for
4. The sender's address ... in the top right-hand corner.
   a. comes — c. goes
   b. is belonging — d. places
5. Where do the wine glasses ...? In this cupboard, or in the cupboard in the other room?
   a. come to — c. go
   b. come — d. stay
6. We had a very long discussion, but I'm afraid we ... far.
   a. didn't come — c. didn't get
   b. didn't cover — d. didn't reach
7. Christmas ... soon.
   a. comes — c. is going to be
   b. is arriving — d. will be here
8. Regina ... hospital next week for an operation.
   a. is coming into — c. comes to the
   b. is going to — d. will be coming into
9. ... while I was having my shower this morning.
   a. A great idea came — c. I became a great idea
   b. A great idea came me — d. I had a great idea
10. I've put on over six kilos. That ... eating too much and getting too little exercise.
    a. is because — c. comes of
    b. comes from — d. goes from

1	2	3	4	5	6	7	8	9	10

A4 I'm looking for ... *Karte / card*

Ergänzen Sie eine passende Entsprechung für „Karte".

1. At a kiosk

◆ Yes, please?

● I'm looking for a ________ of the south of England. Not just a plan of London, but the whole of the south of the country.

2. At a restaurant

◆ Was everything all right?

● Yes, it was very nice, thank you.

◆ Would you like a dessert?

● Yes, can we see the ________ again, please?

3. At a theatre booking office

◆ Yes, please?

● I would like three ________s for tomorrow evening's performance, please.

4. In a shop

◆ Isn't it Anna's birthday next week?

● Yes. I must get her a ________.

5. At a station

◆ Excuse me, can you help me with this machine? I want to buy a ________ to go to the city centre.

● That's Zone A. Just press this button here.

A5 Coming and going *gehen / go*

Wählen Sie die richtige(n) Lösung(en), um die Übersetzung zu vervollständigen.

1. Es ist nicht weit, ich gehe zu Fuß.
   It's not far, I'm going ... .

   ○ (kein weiteres Wort). ○ by foot ○ to walk

2. Wie lange geht die Sendung?
   How long does the programme ...?

   ○ go ○ last ○ take

3. Wo gehen die Kinder zur Schule?
   Where do the children ...?

   ○ go to school ○ go in school ○ walk to school

4. Die Heizung geht nicht.
   The heating ... .

   ○ doesn't go ○ doesn't function ○ isn't working

5. Wann geht Ihre Maschine?
   When ...?

   ○ is your flight ○ does your plane go ○ does your flight go

6. Geht der Bus auch sonntags?
   Does the bus ... on Sundays too?

   ○ drive ○ run ○ travel

7. Das kommt nicht in Frage. Das geht nicht.
   That's out of the question. ...

   ○ That's not going ○ That's impossible. ○ I can't make it.

A6 **Oh damn!** *vergessen / forget*

Welches Verb ist richtig?

1. ... the name of the street.
   a. He's forgotten   b. He's left
2. ... the piece of paper with the address on at home!
   a. He's forgotten   b. He's left
3. Jack is impossible! ... his PIN again!
   a. He's forgotten   b. He's left
4. Oh no! ... my mobile in the car!
   a. I've forgotten   b. I've left
5. There's big trouble. Williams ... the CD with all the data on the train!
   a. has forgotten   b. has left

A7 **What is it?** *Glas / glass*

Ergänzen Sie. Sie können die angegebenen Wörter mehrmals verwenden.

glass • honey • jar • of • olives • wine

1.
a ____________________

2.
a ____________________

3.
a ____________________

4.
a ____________________

A8 A crossword *Salat, Soße / salad, sauce*

Ergänzen Sie passende Übersetzungen von „Salat" und „Soße".

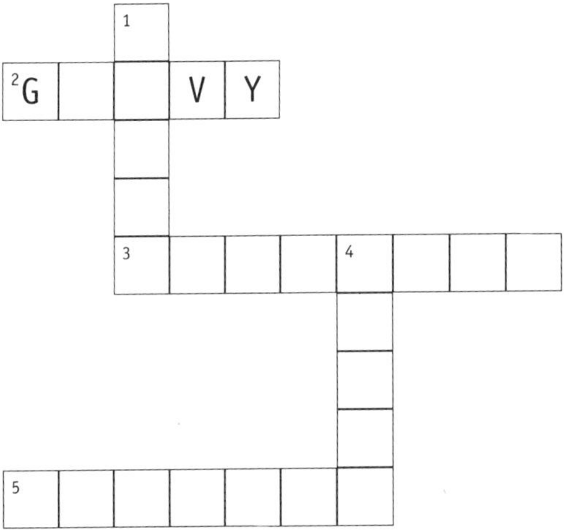

1. This dish is served with French fries and vegetables, or French fries and ... . You can help yourself from the ... bar.
2. I never make ... out of a packet, I always use the meat juices from cooking.
3. What sort of ... do you want on your salad? Italian or French?
4. One of my favourite desserts is ice-cream with chocolate ... .
5. We grow our own ... in the garden.

A9 In the kitchen *scharf / sharp*

Ergänzen Sie passende Übersetzungen von „scharf".

1. One of the most important pieces of kitchen equipment is a set of __________ knives.
2. Glenn likes ___________ food – curries, anything with chili powder or Tabasco sauce!

A10 **Definitions** *Gast / guest*

Ordnen Sie zu.

customer • guest • guesthouse • host • inn
passenger • visitor

1. When you visit someone in their home, you are that person's ____________.
2. They are your ____________.
3. If they have a room especially for people who come and stay overnight, that is their ____________ room.
4. When you eat in a restaurant, you are one of the restaurant's ____________s.
5. When you stay in a hotel, you are a hotel ____________.
6. When you spend some time in another country, you are a ____________ to that country.
7. When you travel in a taxi, you are the taxi driver's ____________.
8. The place where you go for a drink or a meal with friends, and where you can also stay the night is called an ____________.
9. A ____________ is a sort of small private hotel.

A11 **Life-long learning** *lernen / learn*

Korrigieren Sie – falls nötig!

1. I've decided that I'm going to *learn* _________ Spanish.
2. Angela is upstairs in her room *learning* _________. She has a history test tomorrow.
3. Some people just never *learn* _________ .

A12 The test was easy *falsch / false*

Ergänzen Sie *false* oder *wrong*.

1. The test was easy, it consisted of just twenty true-__________ questions.
2. I'm sorry, but your answer is __________.
3. There's no need to worry, it was a __________ alarm.
4. I went to the __________ address.
5. The man gave the police a __________ address, but they soon found out.
6. I only got one question __________, all my other answers were correct.
7. The driver of the other car was on the __________ side of the road. That's why the accident happened.
8. I couldn't understand what I had done __________.
9. I felt such a fool. I had arrived on the __________ day!
10. This class is one for real beginners. If you already know some English, you should register for the __________ beginners' class.

A13 Time for coffee *Pause / pause*

Übersetzen Sie.

1. Um 15.00 Uhr machen wir eine Kaffeepause.
   We'll ______________________________ at three o'clock.
2. Es gab eine kurze Pause, nicht mehr als zwei Sekunden.
   ______________________________, not more than two seconds.
3. Das Theaterstück war sehr lang und es gab zwei Pausen.
   ____
4. An manchen Tagen habe ich so viel zu tun, dass ich keine Mittagspause mache.
   ____
5. Hören Sie zu und sprechen Sie in der Pause nach.
   ____
6. Die [Schul-]Pause ist nach der zweiten [Unterrichts-]Stunde.
   ____

A14 A visit to a castle *dick / thick*

Was ist richtig: a oder b? Oder sind a und b beide richtig?

The castle was really impressive, with walls nearly three metres (a.) fat / (b.) thick (1.). One of the most interesting things about it was that it had a library, with some beautiful old leather books, really (a.) fat / (b.) thick (2.) books that must have been very valuable. We had just finished our tour and were just coming out of the front gate, when a (a.) big fat / (b.) thick (3.) car drove up. It stopped, and a man got out. He was small, but incredibly (a.) fat / (b.) thick (4.). He walked round to the other side of the car, opened the door, and a woman got out. 'Welcome to Wellesborne', he said, and gave her a (a.) big / (b.) thick (5.) kiss on her cheek. She didn't like this at all, it was clearly a (a.) big / (b.) thick (6.) mistake. But it didn't seem to bother him. He laughed and said something to the gatekeeper, who then laughed too. They were obviously (a.) close / (b.) thick (7.) friends.

1	2	3	4	5	6	7

A15 Some things are extra *extra / extra*

Übersetzen Sie. Verwenden Sie die angegebenen Ausdrücke.

extra • on purpose • separately • specially

1. Kostet das extra?

   ____

2. Ich bezahle den Wein extra.

   ____

3. Ich habe den Wein extra für dich gekauft.

   ____

4. Er hat es extra gemacht, ich bin sicher!

   ____

A16 Not long, but ... *lang / long*

Ergänzen Sie. Nicht alle angegebenen Wörter werden benötigt.

a long time • for • length • long • twenty years

1. I waited ______________, it was almost an hour.
2. ____________________ they've been going to the same place for their holidays, every year the same.
3. It was the shoulder-___________ hair that made me think it was a woman.
4. The journey time is the same ___________, whether you go by car or by train.
5. I haven't seen them for ______________, it must be over five years since we last met.

A17 **Young athletes** *Preis / price, prize*

Was ist richtig: a oder b?

Some of these gymnasts are very young, not more than 14 or 15 years old. They may win a lot of (a.) prices / (b.) prizes (1.), but they pay a high (a.) price / (b.) prize (2.).

A18 **Ears open** *(zu)hören / hear*

Ergänzen Sie die passende Form von *hear* oder *listen (to)*.

1. _______ you _______ the latest news? Another bank is in trouble.
2. I'm sorry, can you say that again? I'm afraid I wasn't _________________.
3. The train was full, but I just closed my eyes and _________________ music on my MP3 player.
4. They were shouting at each other. I should think the whole house could _________________ them.
5. I don't know how many times I've told him not to park outside our gate, but he just won't _________________!
6. _________________ closely, and you'll _________________ the difference.

A19 Is it true? *sagen / say*

Ergänzen Sie *say* oder *tell.*

1. Will you please _______ me the truth.
2. Can you _______ me the way to the station?
3. Can you _______ that again, please?
4. _______ hello.
5. I'll _______ them where they can park.
6. _______ us that joke about the DJ again.

A20 What people say *sagen / say*

Übersetzen Sie.

1. Können Sie mir sagen, was es kostet?

   ____

2. Ich sage immer die Wahrheit.

   ____

3. Sie sagte *Happy birthday,* aber es war nicht mein Geburtstag.

   ____

4. Sie ist eine sehr stille Person. Sie sagt nicht viel.

   ____

5. Was hat er euch gesagt?

   ____

6. Was hat er gesagt?

   ____

7. Er sagte, er könnte uns nichts sagen.

   ____

8. Das [Fussball-]Spiel war langweilig. – Das kannst du laut sagen!

   ____

A21 Everything under control *Kontrolle / control*

Ergänzen Sie passende Übersetzungen von „kontrollieren/Kontrolle".

1. He was driving too fast and lost _________ of the car on a bend.
2. Remember to pack the scissors in your suitcase. If you put them in your hand luggage, they'll take them away when you get to the security _________.
3. I work in the quality _________ department.
4. It's all right, there's no need to worry. I have everything under _________.
5. We travelled over 300 kilometres and our tickets were not _________ once.
6. Our work is _________ all the time – it's like working in a police state!
7. The authorities carry out random _________s of restaurants to ensure that health standards are maintained.

A22 Entertaining a visitor *Koch, kochen / cook*

Drei der *kursiv* gedruckten Ausdrücke sind falsch. Korrigieren Sie sie.

◆ Come in, then we can carry on talking while I (1.) *cook* _________ us some tea.

● You have a very nice (2.) *kitchen* _________. I like all this wood.

◆ Thank you.

● Do you (3.) *do much cooking* _________?

◆ No, I don't have time. Brian is the (4.) *cook* _________ in this house. Well, most of the time. At any rate, he gets home first, so he normally (5.) *cooks* _________ our evening meal.

● People always say that English (6.) *kitchen* _________ is not very good. But I don't agree. I've always found that ...

◆ Oh, the water (7.) *is cooking* _________. Excuse me a moment.

A23 A question of how you feel *warm / warm*

Ergänzen Sie *warm* oder *hot*.

1. a nice ____________ day in spring

2. a ____________-water bottle

3. a ____________ meal

4. a terribly ____________ day

5. ____________ and cold water

6. a nice ____________ bath

A24 A breath of fresh air *frisch / fresh*

Ergänzen Sie.

bright • clean • chilly • fresh • wet

1. I need to get some _________ air.
2. We sat outside till ten in the evening, but then it got quite _________ and so we went inside.
3. After a day's hard work it's good to have a shower and put on some _________ clothes.
4. The place was decorated in nice _________ colours.
5. Careful! _________ paint!

A25 The minimum *null / nil*

Ergänzen Sie.

nil • nought • oh • zero

1. It was a hard-fought match which neither team deserved to lose, so it was right that it finished _________ _________.
2. We had the first frost of the winter last night, the temperature is now just one degree above _________.
3. She broke the world record, but only by point _________ one (0,01) of a second!
4. My mobile number is _________ one five seven, ...
5. In a recession the rate of economic growth drops below _________.

A26 Josh's accident *nächste(r/s), neu / next, new*

Ergänzen Sie passende Wörter.

◆ Have you heard the (1.) _________ news?
● No, why? What's happened?
◆ Josh has crashed his (2.) _________ car.
● But he only got it last week.
◆ I know. It was the very (3.) _________ model and must have cost him I don't know how much.
● How did it happen?
◆ Someone stopped him and asked the way to the (4.) _________ bank, so he said, "I'll drive you there, it's only just round the corner." And it was, just round the corner, but they didn't get there because Josh overlooked a red light.
● (5.) _________ time he'll know better than to show off to strangers.

A27 More on cars *Motor / motor*

Wählen Sie die richtige Lösung, a oder b.

We had a terrible journey back from Scotland. It was raining, but the windscreen wipers weren't working properly. There was something wrong with the electric (a.) engine / (b.) motor (1.). We stopped and got that repaired, but then in the middle of a wild stretch of countryside the car broke down completely. This time, it was something major to do with the (a.) engine / (b.) motor (2.).

1	2

A28 All the latest *Technik / technique*

Ergänzen Sie *technique* oder *technology*.

1. In this course you will learn an important new marketing ________.
2. There have been huge advances in medical ________ over the last 50 years.
3. Roberta has a new trainer, and her ________ has improved enormously. She's developing into a first-class player.
4. The company fell behind because it didn't invest in new ________.

A29 Light and dark *Schatten / shade, shadow*

Was ist richtig: a oder b?

1. It's too hot in the sun. Let's try and find a table in the (a.) shade / (b.) shadow.
2. As the sun began to go down behind us, our (a.) shades / (b.) shadows on the lawn[1] grew longer and longer.
3. The news of Will's heart attack cast[2] a (a.) shade / (b.) shadow over the whole evening.
4. He's now only a (a.) shade / (b.) shadow of the man he used to be.
5. After lunch, I lay down and slept in the (a.) shade / (b.) shadow of a big chestnut tree[3].

1	2	3	4	5

[1]Rasen [2]warf [3]Kastanienbaum

A30 **And so to bed** *schlafen / sleep*

Was ist richtig: a oder b? Oder sind a und b beide richtig?

1. Sleep researchers have found that we now (a.) are asleep / (b.) sleep over an hour less than fifty years ago.
2. Fifty years ago people were often in bed and (a.) asleep / (b.) sleeping by ten thirty in the evening.
3. It's been a long day and I think it's time for me to go to (a.) bed / (b.) sleep. Goodnight everybody and thanks for a wonderful evening.
4. I'm sorry I disturbed you. I didn't realize you were (a.) asleep / (b.) sleeping.
5. Most nights I switch the light off and (a.) am asleep / (b.) sleep within ten minutes.
6. Sometimes I wake in the middle of the night and have problems (a.) getting back to sleep / (b.) falling asleep again.
7. I'm not one of these people who sleep (a.) in / (b.) late at the weekend. I still get up quite early.
8. The presentation was so boring, the speaker's voice so monotonous that it (a.) brought / (b.) sent me to sleep.

1	2	3	4	5	6	7	8

A31 **Opinion poll results** *Politik / politics, policy*

Ergänzen Sie *politics, policy* oder *policies.*

1. In the opinion poll, over 30% of young people said they weren't interested in _________.
2. In the same poll, over 50% of all respondents said they were dissatisfied with the government's economic _________.
3. As always, the US presidential election seems to be more about personalities. It's not clear what _________ each candidate has on the major issues facing the country.

A32 **In the media** *Programm / programme, program*

Übersetzen Sie.

1. Sie hatten kein Satellitenfernsehen und es gab nur drei Programme.
   ____
2. Es gibt viele Verbesserungen in der neuen Version des [Computer-]Programms.
   ____
3. Das Festivalprogramm ist nun erschienen.
   ____
4. Welches [TV-]Programm schauen Sie am meisten?
   ____

A33 **Not always a house** *Haus / house*

Korrigieren Sie – falls nötig!

1. I'm sorry, but Herr Werner is out of the *house* __________. Try calling back this afternoon.
2. Ann and Steve have just sold their *house* __________.
3. The hospital always sends a report to your *house doctor* __________.
4. The teacher gives a lot of work to be done at *house* __________.

A34 What do you mean? *meinen / mean*

Korrigieren Sie – falls nötig.

1. What do you *mean by* ______________ "very expensive"?
2. When I said, "he's too old", I *didn't mean* ______________ you.
3. I *mean* __________ it's a good idea. What's your view?
4. I'm sorry. I *didn't mean* _____________ to hurt you.
5. I agree with you entirely. I *mean* ___________ exactly the same.

A35 Getting it right *Komma / comma*

Ergänzen Sie eine passende Übersetzung von „Komma".

1. The increase was minimal, just nought _______________ seven per cent.
2. In German you always put a __________ before *dass*, but in English you never put one before 'that'.

A36 What do you want? (1) *wollen / want*

Welche Verbform ist richtig?

1. We got to the station just as the train ... leave.
   a. wanted to b. was about to
2. Lots of migrants ... America.
   a. want to b. want to get to
3. Damn! The car ... start.
   a. doesn't want to b. won't
4. There we were, ready to leave, and the car ... start.
   a. didn't want to b. wouldn't

1	2	3	4

A37 What do you want? (2) *wollen / want*

Übersetzen Sie.

1. Wen wollen Sie sprechen?

   ____
2. Ich wollte gerade gehen, als Jim anrief.

   ____
3. Der Besucher will zu Mr Smith.

   ____
4. Ich will ins Bett.

   ____
5. Ich hab's ihr hundert Mal gesagt, aber sie will einfach nicht hören.

   I've told her a hundred times, but ____________________
6. Ich versuchte das Fenster zu öffnen, aber es wollte nicht.

   ____
7. Moment mal! Was wollen Sie damit sagen?! Dass ich ein Dieb bin?!

   Just a moment! ____________________? That I'm a thief?!

A38 Your money *Kosten, kosten / cost[s]*

Ergänzen Sie passende Übersetzungen von „kosten/Kosten".

1. The ________ of petrol rose last year by over 15%.
2. Will we save on production ________ by introducing the new technology? That's the key question.
3. The ________ of living in London will be a real shock for them when they move there.
4. It will ________ too much time. We'll have to abandon the idea.
5. Money doesn't seem to be a problem. He wants to go so much that he's prepared to go at his own ________.
6. How much will it ________ to park at the airport?

A39 Help! *helfen / help*

Ergänzen Sie die Übersetzung. Verwenden Sie die vorgegebenen Wörter.

It's • do • for • good • is • no • one • only
There's • thing • to • use

1. Es hilft nichts. Wir müssen ganz von vorne anfangen.
   ________________. We're going to have to start all over again.
2. Honig mit Zitrone hilft gegen Halsschmerzen.
   Honey with lemon ________________. a sore throat.
3. Da hilft nur eins: alle Banken verstaatlichen.
   ________________: nationalize all the banks.

A40 **Lots of people** *Publikum, publik / public*

Ist das *kursiv* gesetzte Wort richtig oder falsch?

1. It's an absolute scandal. This needs to be made *public*.
2. At the end of the play the *public* gave the actors a standing ovation.

A41 **It's natural** *Natur / nature*

Ergänzen Sie die Übersetzungen.

1. Am Wochenende bin ich gern in der freien Natur.
   At the weekend I like to be out in the ________________.
2. Es liegt in der menschlichen Natur, Fehler zu machen.
   It's h______ ________ to make mistakes.
3. Pflanzen, Tiere, Menschen: wir alle sind Teil der Natur.
   Plants, animals, human beings: we are all part of __________.

A42 **Is it OK?** *wenn / when*

Ergänzen Sie *when* oder *if*.

1. Is it OK _________ we meet a little bit later?
2. We can discuss everything else _________ we meet.
3. I'll let you know _________ the flight arrives.
4. _________ you need any help, just ask.
5. _________ things continue like this, we'll have to take some drastic action.
6. I'll only phone _________ there's a problem.
7. Start without us _________ we're late. Don't wait.
8. _________ we finish, I'll take them on a guided tour.
9. _________ we finish early, I'll fill in time by taking them on a guided tour.

A43 What can you say? *Menü, Appetit, grillen / ...*

Kreuzen Sie alle korrekten Sätze an.

1.
a. I'll have today's menu, please.
b. I'll have today's special, please.
c. I'll have today's set meal, please.

2.
a. Here you are, sir. Enjoy your meal.
b. Here you are, sir. Bon appétit.
c. Here you are, sir. Good appetite.

3.
a. It's a beautiful evening for a grill.
b. It's a beautiful evening for a barbecue.
c. It's a beautiful evening to grill.
d. It's a beautiful evening to have a grill party.

A44 Plans and activities *Aktion / action*

Welcher Ausdruck passt in die Lücke?

1. Which products are we going to place at the centre of our summer advertising ...?
   a. action b. campaign
2. We already have a provisional plan of ... .
   a. action b. campaign
3. There has been more military ... in Northern Afghanistan.
   a. action b. campaign
4. A number of different charities have launched ... to help the victims of the earthquake.
   a. an action b. a campaign

A45 Criminal activity *rauben / rob*

Kreuzen Sie die richtige Lösung an.

	rob	steal	
1.	○	○	a bank
2.	○	○	jewels from someone's house
3.	○	○	priceless paintings from a museum
4.	○	○	somebody on the underground
5.	○	○	a team of what seemed certain victory
6.	○	○	a star of her diamond ring
7.	○	○	the tomb of an Egyptian king
8.	○	○	stationery from the office
9.	○	○	€ 3 million from an online bank account
10.	○	○	people of their life savings

A46 **Not always high** *hoch / high*

Übersetzen Sie.

1. Es war kalt und wir hatten hohen Schnee.

   ____

2. Santa Claus wohnt im hohen Norden.

   ____

3. Es war Hochsommer und das Gras war hoch.

   ____

4. Wie hoch war der Betrag, der gestohlen wurde?

   ____

5. Sie hat eine hoch bezahlte Stelle bei einer Computerfirma.

   ____

6. Die Stadt ist von hohen Bergen umgeben.

   ____

7. Hände hoch!

   ____

8. Der Zug fuhr mit hoher Geschwindigkeit in den Tunnel hinein.

   ____

9. Wir rechnen mit nicht mehr als 30 Personen, wenn es hoch kommt.

   ____

10. Immer mehr Menschen erreichen ein hohes Alter.

    ____

11. Er hat hohe Schulden.

    ____

12. Die Mannschaft hat hoch gewonnen.

    ____

A47 It's chaos at home. *lassen / let*

Was passt in die Lücke? Mehrere Lösungen sind möglich.

1. It's chaos at home. We ... the whole house ...	a. are letting ... repaint b. are letting ... repainted c. are having ... repainted d. are making ... repainted
2. I'm a bit short of time. ... to explain it to you.	a. Let Wanda b. Get Wanda c. Ask Wanda d. Make Wanda
3. They ... over half an hour.	a. kept us waiting b. made us wait c. let us to wait d. made us to wait
4. ...! You know I don't like it.	a. Let that b. Leave that c. Let that be d. Stop that
5. Can you just ..., please?!	a. let me b. leave me alone c. leave me to be d. leave me work
6. Can you ... for everyone, please?	a. let copies make b. have copies made c. make copies to be made d. make it be copied

Und nun übersetzen Sie.

7. Robin und Ann lassen euch grüßen.

____

A48 On the road (1) *Straße / street*

Ergänzen Sie *road* oder *street*.

1. a ____________________

2. a ____________________

3. A __________ is what cars, buses etc. use to get from A to B.
4. A __________ is a place where people live, work, go shopping, etc.

A49 On the road (2) *Straße / street*

Kreuzen Sie die richtige Lösung an.

	road	street	
1.	○	○	Excuse me. Is this the ... to Inverness?
2.	○	○	How much crime is there? How safe are the ...s in this part of town?
3.	○	○	The private detective stood on the ... corner reading a newspaper.
4.	○	○	Drivers need to take extra care on the ...s this morning. There is a lot of fog about.
5.	○	○	He was driving far too fast and came off the ... .
6.	○	○	The country ... is best if you want to enjoy the scenery.
7.	○	○	The exhibition centre is on the ... to Walsall.
8.	○	○	The major shopping ...s are to the west of the station.

A50 **Welcome to Wembley ...** *Stadium / stadium*

Was passt in die Lücke?

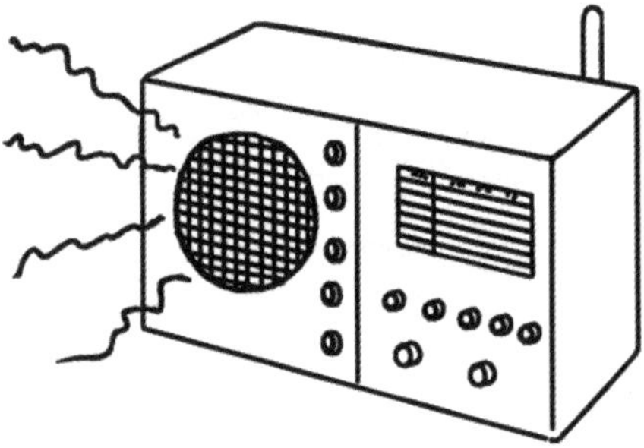

Welcome back to Wembley (1.) ..., where the second half of this important qualifying match is already well under way.
At this (2.) ... of the game, ten minutes into the second half, the match is wide open, and either team could win.

1.

a. sports centre
b. sports ground
c. stadion
d. stadium

2.

a. part
b. event
c. segment
d. stage

A51 Make and do (1) *machen / make*

Kreuzen Sie die richtige Lösung an.

	make	do	
1.	○	○	I can't ... this sudoku. Can you help me?
2.	○	○	What am I to ...? I've tried everything.
3.	○	○	Do you have to ... much overtime in your job?
4.	○	○	We need to ... some decisions.
5.	○	○	If I cook, will you ... the washing up?
6.	○	○	I'm afraid I'm going to ... a mistake.
7.	○	○	I'll ... the shopping on my way home.
8.	○	○	Does it ... any difference what I think?
9.	○	○	What do you ... for a living?
10.	○	○	I'd like to ... a Chinese course.
11.	○	○	I used to ... quite a lot of sport.
12.	○	○	I'd like to ... a suggestion if I may.

A52 Make and do (2) *machen / make*

Übersetzen Sie.

1. Wann machen Sie in diesem Jahr Urlaub?
   ____
2. Warte, ich will ein Foto machen.
   ____
3. Es macht nichts.
   ____
4. Sollen wir Pause machen?
   ____
5. Ich mache Diät.
   ____
6. Wann machen Sie Ihre Prüfung?
   ____
7. Mach dir keine Sorgen.
   ____

A53 Make and do (3) *machen / make*

Ergänzen Sie die richtige(n) Verbform(en).

1. The engine ... a funny noise. I think we should stop and see what's wrong.

   ● is doing ● is making

2. In German dogs ... *wau wau,* but in English 'woof woof'.

   ● do ● go ● make

3. On Sunday afternoons we always had to ... a walk. It was awful.

   ● do ● go for ● make

4. I only ... four questions right.

   ● did ● got ● made

5. It's not ideal, but let's ... the best of it.

   ● do ● make

6. I'm ... my best.

   ● doing ● making

7. Let's ... a start, we have a lot to get through.

   ● do ● get ● make

8. Can you ... me a favour?

   ● do ● give ● make

9. Quite a number of employees ... a little sleep during the lunch break.

   ● do ● have ● make

10. You've ... a really good job. Thank you very much indeed.

    ● done ● made

11. At school I used to like ... translations.

    ● doing ● making

B. False friends

Englisch-deutsche Wortpaare mit ähnlicher Form aber unterschiedlicher Bedeutung

B1 Globalization *Fabrik / fabric*

Kreuzen Sie die richtige(n) Antwort(en) an.

The company I used to work for produces (1.) ... for the furniture industry, for sofas, beds, etc. They used to have (2.) ... in western Europe, but now most of the production is based in Rumania. When the company relocated, many people lost their jobs.

1. a. cloths
   b. fabrics
   c. materials
   d. stuffs

2. a. fabrics
   b. factories
   c. production places
   d. workplaces

B2 What makes a good film? *Kritik / critic*

Richtig oder falsch? Wenn falsch, wie lautet der richtige Ausdruck?

- ● Did you enjoy the film?
- ◆ I did. Films that have a (1.) *happy end* __________ make you feel good.
- ● That doesn't mean they are good films.
- ◆ You sound like one of these film (2.) *critics* __________. Anyway. Have you read the (3.) *critic* __________ of the film in the paper?

B3 Please fill it in. *Formular / formula*

Ergänzen Sie *form* oder *formula*.

1. Can you please fill in this __________?
2. What is your __________ for success?
3. This weekend is the last race in this year's __________ One series.
4. What's the mathematical __________ for calculating the area of a circle?
5. Support in the __________ of cash is also very welcome.

B4 In a café *überhören / overhear*

Was passt in die Lücke? Mehrere Lösungen sind möglich.

> As I was sitting in the café waiting for Minako, I (1.) ... two men at the next table talking about a "delivery at midnight", and I thought I heard the word 'cocaine'. I tried to catch what else they were saying. I was listening so intently to their conversation that I (2.) ... my mobile ringing. It was Minako calling to say she'd be late.

1. a. became with
   b. happened to hear
   c. overheard
   d. overcame

2. a. didn't hear
   b. failed to hear
   c. heard over
   d. overheard

B5 Times are changing *Branche, Chef, Personal, ... / ...*

Ergänzen Sie.

1. Banks used to have b _ _ _ _ _ _ s in every town.
2. Companies in our b _ _ _ _ _ _ s are really feeling the recession.
3. There has been another big t _ k _ _ _ _ r. The second biggest bank in the country has bought up the fourth biggest.
4. We were going so slowly that even people on bikes o _ _ _ _ _ _ k us!
5. The company has been forced to cut costs and reduce s _ _ _ _.
6. PIN stands for _ _ _ _ _ _ _ _ identification number.
7. A firm that organizes funerals[1] is called an u _ _ e _ _ _ _ _ r.
8. Bill Gates must be seen as one of the great ent _ _ pr _ _ eurs of the 20th century.
9. How are you getting on with your new b _ _ s?
10. A _ _ _ _ works in a restaurant and plans and cooks meals.

[1]Beerdingungen

B6 Don't just sit there! *Rückseite / backside*

Was passt in die Lücke? Mehrere Lösungen sind möglich.

Mother	Don't just sit there on your (1.) ...! Get up and do something.
Son	What?
Mother	Well, for a start you can go and get the rest of the shopping out of the car.
Son	Where is it?
Mother	Parked (2.) ... of the building where it always is!

1. a. backside
   b. behind
   c. bottom
   d. sit

2. a. at the back side
   b. at the back
   c. on the back side
   d. on the back

B7 Definitions *selbstbewusst, sensibel, sympathisch / ...*

Ordnen Sie zu.

pleasant • self-conscious • self-confident
sensible • sensitive • sympathetic

1. Someone who is ______________ is often nervous and worries about what other people think of them.
2. A ______________ person is the opposite of the type of person described in sentence 1. This sort of person feels good about him or herself.
3. A ______________ person is someone who is practical and makes wise decisions.
4. If you are ______________ you have good antennae for how other people feel, you can put yourself in their situation and understand how they feel.
5. If you like another person, you find them nice or ______________.
6. A ______________ person listens carefully to your worries and cares about your problems.

B8 I prefer people like you and me *ordinär / ordinary*

Was passt in die Lücke? Mehrere Lösungen sind möglich.

Mr Bagshot may have lots of money and lots of friends in high places, but I find him distinctly (1.) … . He's always telling jokes and stories that are in bad taste. I prefer normal, (2.) … people – people like you and me!

1. a. common
   b. orderly
   c. out of the ordinary
   d. vulgar

2. a. ordinal
   b. every day
   c. ordinary
   d. usual

B9 What is what? *Keks / cake*

Ergänzen Sie.

1. a ______________________________

2. a ______________________________

B10 What do you think? *Meinung / meaning*

Korrigieren Sie.

◆ What do you think of the new proposals that have been put forward by the government?

● I'm sceptical. What's your *meaning* ___________?

B11 Have you got your results? *Note, Notiz / note, notice*

Ergänzen Sie *note, notice* oder einen anderen passenden Ausdruck.

1. I hear that you've got your exam results. What ___________ did you get? – An A in English, and a C in German.
2. I have to write a summary of the meeting, but there's one topic where the ___________s I took are not clear.
3. I must make a mental ___________ of that so that I don't forget.
4. When he got home he found a ___________ on the kitchen table saying she was gone.
5. The best thing to do is to ignore him. Just don't take any ___________.
6. There was a big ___________ on the gate saying 'Please do not feed the animals'.
7. I carry a little ___________book round with me in which I write down all the new words I hear. It's a good way to learn new vocabulary.
8. I can sing OK, but I can't read ___________. I have to learn new songs by listening.

B12 **Things that arrive** *bekommen / become*

Welcher Satz ist richtig?

1.
a. I become the quiche, please.
b. I get the quiche, please.
c. I have the quiche, please.
d. I'll have the quiche, please.

2.
a. Fran has become a baby
b. Fran got a baby.
c. Fran has had a baby.
d. Fran has received a baby.

B13 **What the postman brings** *Paket / packet*

Übersetzen Sie.

1. Wann holt der Kurier die Pakete ab?
   ____
2. Die Regierung hat ein Maßnahmenpaket bewilligt.
   The government has approved ______________________
3. Ich benutze mehrere Softwarepakete von Microsoft.
   ____
4. Zwei Päckchen Butter und ein Päckchen Tee.
   ____

B14 Different concepts *Konzept / concept*

Ist der *kursiv* gedruckte Ausdruck richtig oder falsch? Wenn falsch, korrigieren Sie ihn.

1. The *concept* _________ of 'democracy' goes back to ancient Greece.
2. I've completed the first *concept* _________ of my dissertation, but it is still very rough and needs more work done on it.
3. The marketing *concept* _________ for the new brand includes a whole range of activities and measures.
4. The question completely *brought him out of his concept* _________________.

B15 This and that *Mappe, Tablett, Fotograf / map, tablet, ...*

Beschriften Sie die Bilder.

folder • map • photograph • photographer
tablet • tray

1. a _________

2. a _________

3. a _________

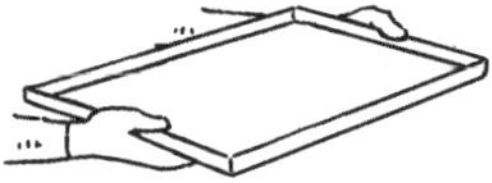

4. a _________

5. a _________

6. a _________

316 Killed by a cup of tea *Mörder, Gift / murder, gift*
Ergänzen Sie.

gift • murder • murderer • poison

Police are investigating the bizarre (1.) __________ of an old lady in an old people's home. It seems that the (2.) __________ killed his or her victim by putting some (3.) __________ into the old lady's early-morning tea. It was her birthday, and she had received a number of cards and (4.) __________.

317 What's on a piece of paper *Rezept / receipt*
Übersetzen Sie.

1. Ich bezahlte und der Taxifahrer gab mir eine Quittung.

   ____

2. Es schmeckt wunderbar. Du musst mir das Rezept geben.

   ____

3. Das Rezept muss noch von der Ärztin unterschrieben werden.

   ____

4. Was ist Ihr Erfolgsrezept?

   ____

B18 **Hard times** *Rente / rent*

Was passt in die Lücke? Mehrere Lösungen sind möglich.

1. More and more old people are finding it hard to survive on the state ... .

   a. pay
   b. pension
   c. retirement money
   d. old-age allowance

2. She'll be 66 next March and will be ... .

   a. going to rent
   b. going into retirement
   c. retiring
   d. going to rest

3. My flat has become too expensive. My landlord[1] put up the ... again.

   a. monthly fee
   b. money
   c. rent
   d. tax

B19 **Actually, no ...** *aktuell / actual*

Ergänzen Sie jeweils die passende Entsprechung von „aktuell".

1. ◆ You can't go by that timetable. It's no longer v _ _ _ _.
   ● Sorry?
   ◆ It's no longer u_ to d _ _ _.
2. ◆ Hunault's latest book is set in the present day and is about the winners and losers of globalization.
   ● So it's very t _ _ _ _ _ _.
3. ◆ What's in the news?
   ● The same thing as last week and the week before. All the media are full of the c _ _ _ _ _ _ _ crisis in the banking sector.

[1]Vermieter

B20 **Money matters** *sparen, spenden / spare, spend*

Ergänzen Sie (eine passende Form von) *save, spare, spend* oder *donate*.

1. Can you __________ me ten minutes? I'd like to ask you for some advice.
2. It'll __________ time and help to keep the meeting short if you arrange it for quite late in the afternoon.
3. I got €300 out of the bank this morning and I've __________ it all already. I'm not very good at managing my money.
4. When the economic climate cools down, people __________ less to charity.
5. You can __________ a few euros if you book online. It's slightly cheaper.

B21 **An accident** *übersehen, Handy, blinken / oversee, ...*

Korrigieren Sie.

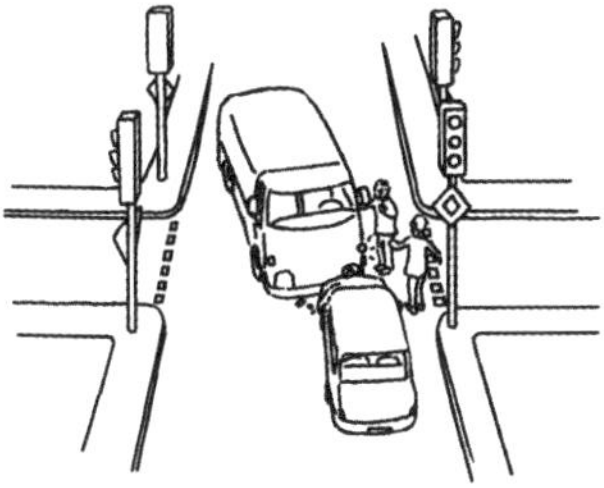

This is how the accident happened. The driver of the delivery van was on his (1.) ~~handy~~ __________ and not paying attention to what was happening on the road. He wanted to turn left, and had (2.) ~~blinked~~ __________ left, but he (3.) ~~oversaw~~ __________ the car coming the other way.
It all happened in the *blink* of an eye, very quickly indeed. There were plenty of other witnesses[1] besides me because I *was overseeing* a group of students who were doing a photography project. It was *handy* that they all had cameras.

[1]Zeugen

B22 Children *brav, Gymnasium, Mobbing / brave, gymnasium, …*

Was passt in die Lücke? Mehrere Lösungen sind möglich.

1.
◆ Our usual babysitter goes to the same school as Tina.
● Which school is that?
◆ The local ...

a. gymnasium
b. second school
c. grammar school
d. higher school

2.
● Is that a good school?
◆ Yes, we're very happy. There don't seem to be any problems with ... or anything like that.

a. bullying
b. harassers
c. mobbing
d. mobbsters

3.
◆ Has everything been OK?
● Yes, the children have been very ..., no problem at all. They went to bed when I told them to, did exactly what I asked them to do.
◆ They're not like that with us, I can assure you!

a. brave
b. good
c. bold
d. well-behaved

B23 Keeping fit *Gymnastik, wandern / gymnastics, wander*

Ergänzen Sie *exercises*, *gymnastics*, *hiking* oder *wandering*. Benutzen Sie jedes Wort nur einmal.

1. ____________ is an Olympic discipline. Some of the best athletes are still children.
2. I'm not one of these people who get out of bed in the morning and do their keep-fit ____________.
3. I had an hour to spare, so I spent it ____________ round the old town.
4. Autumn is the best time to go ____________ in the mountains.

B24 The weekend paper *Prospekt, Annonce / prospect, ...*
Ergänzen Sie.

advertisement • announcements • brochures • prospects

The first thing I do when I get the weekend paper is to sort out and throw away all the bits I'm not interested in. These include all the separate advertising (1.) __________ and all the (2.) __________ sections for jobs, housing, cars, etc.

The paper is still then very thick, and my (3.) __________ of getting through all of it very slim. So another thing I don't read is the section with all the birth, marriage and death (4.) __________.

B25 In the air *gründen / ground*
Ergänzen Sie *founded* oder *grounded*.

British Airways was (1.) __________ in 1974, when the two companies BOAC (British Overseas Airways Corporation) and BEA (British European Airways) were merged. BOAC had previously been (2.) __________, when British Airways and Imperial Airways were merged in 1937.
As you can see, today we have thick fog here at the airport, and most of the fleet[1] has been (3.) __________ .

[1]Flotte

B26 **Not now, but ...** *eventuell / eventually*

Wählen Sie den Ausdruck oder die Ausdrücke mit der gleichen Bedeutung wie *eventually*.

1. The train *eventually* arrived, over 45 minutes late.

   ○ sometime ○ at last ○ finally ○ one day

2. *Eventually* all this will belong to you, son.

   ○ sometime ○ at last ○ finally ○ one day

B27 **Don't wait** *eventuell / eventually*

Wählen Sie alle passenden Übersetzungen.

1. Er kommt eventuell nicht. Wir sollen nicht auf ihn warten.
   a. He may not come. We are not to wait for him.
   b. He possibly won't be coming. We are not to wait for him.
   c. It's possible that he won't be coming. We are not to wait for him.
   d. He likely won't be coming. We are not to wait for him.

2. Wir haben eventuell ein Problem.
   a. We can have a problem.
   b. We possibly have a problem.
   c. We may have a problem.
   d. We have a possible problem.

1	2

B28 What you need to make something *Stoff / stuff*
Ergänzen Sie die Übersetzungen.

1. Aus welchem Stoff ist das Zelt?

   What ___________ is the tent made of?
2. Ich habe Stoff gekauft und werde die Vorhänge selber nähen.

   I've bought some ___________ and am going to make the curtains myself.
3. Es gibt verschiedene chemische Stoffe, die diese Eigenschaft haben.

   There are various chemical ___________ that have this property.
4. Wo findet sie den Stoff für ihre Geschichten?

   Where does she find the ___________ for her stories?

B29 Goods *Warenhaus / warehouse*
Was passt in die Lücken?

Goods are produced, stored in a ... (1), then moved to the place where they are sold – for example, big ...s (2), like KDW in Berlin, Macy's in New York, or Selfridges in London.

a. department store
b. shopping store
c. retail house
d. warehouse

B30 A question of religion *Konfession / confession*

Ergänzen Sie.

belief • confession • denomination • denotation

- ◆ What (1.) __________ are you? Protestant or Roman Catholic?
- ● Roman Catholic. At least on paper.
- ◆ So that means you go to (2.) __________?
- ● Sorry?
- ◆ You go to the priest and tell him what you have done wrong.
- ● Well, I should do, or would do if I was a practising Roman Catholic.

B31 Wedding bells *engagiert / engaged*

Sortieren Sie die Buchstaben.

1. Laura and Michael have just got *G A N E G E D* ________________. The wedding is going to take place next March.
2. Laura is a teacher. She's very *T E A D D E D I C* _________________ to her job.
3. Michael is a social worker. He's also very *T E M O M C I T D* ______________________ to his work.
4. Both of them are heavily *V O N E V D I L* ____________________ in the anti-globalization movement.
5. They are a politically and socially *I V E C A T* _______________ couple.
6. So please don't tell them that I've just been *D E R I H* _______________ by one of the big multi-nationals!

C. Lots of friends

Deutsche Wörter mit mehreren englischen Entsprechungen

C1 At a party *Mann, Frau*

Ergänzen Sie die richtige Übersetzung von „Mann“ und „Frau“.

C2 **Here you are.** *bitte*

Was passt zusammen? Ordnen Sie zu.

1. Darf ich mich hierher setzen? – *Bitte schön.*
2. Vielen Dank. – *Bitte schön.*
3. *Bitte schön*, Ihr Schlüssel.
4. Kann ich *bitte* das Salz haben?
5. *Wie bitte*? Ich verstehe leider nicht.

a. Here you are, your key.
b. May I sit here? – Certainly. / Of course. / Please do.
c. Thanks very much. – It's a pleasure. / That's all right. / You're welcome.
d. Sorry? / Pardon? / Excuse me? I'm afraid I don't understand.
e. Can I have the salt please?

C3 **In a German restaurant** *bitte*

Ergänzen Sie den Dialog mit passenden Ausdrücken aus C2.

◆ Excuse me. Do you mind if I join you?
■ Entschuldigung?
◆ May I sit here?
■ Yes, (1.) ______________________.
...
◆ Can I see the menu, please?
● *(Gives the menu.)* (2.) ______________________.
◆ Thanks very much.
Hmm. Interesting. But can you explain what this is, 'xzysxwlm'?
● (3.) ______________________?
◆ Sorry, it's my German pronunciation. I can't say it properly.
● Can I see, (4.) ______________________?
◆ Sure. *(Points to something.)* Here.
● Ah, 'Saumagen'. Well, that's something very, er, special, it's ...
...
◆ Thanks for all your help.
● (5.) ______________________.

C4 A postcard *als*

Ergänzen Sie eine passende Entsprechung für „als".

(1.) ________ we arrived,
it was pouring with rain.
And that's how the holiday
has continued. I don't think
we've had a wetter holiday
(2.) ________ this one!
When people find out that I'm
English, they say, "Well,
(3.) ____________ an
English person you must be used
to this." (4.) __________
if it rained all the time in
England!

C5 Where you go and what you do *besuchen*

Ergänzen Sie eine passende Übersetzung von „besuchen".

attend • go to • visit

1. We're not going away, can't afford a holiday this year. We'll probably take the odd day and go and ____________ friends or relatives.
2. In this country children have to ____________ school until the age of 16.
3. Even if you don't live in the city, you can still enjoy what's on offer culturally, ____________ concerts and things.

C6 **Payment** *(be)zahlen*

Kreuzen Sie die richtige Lösung an.

	pay	pay for	
1.	○	○	taxes
2.	○	○	repairs
3.	○	○	€ 80 for something
4.	○	○	tickets in cash
5.	○	○	€ 18 each for the tickets
6.	○	○	a taxi driver
7.	○	○	a taxi to take someone somewhere
8.	○	○	bills
9.	○	○	a person or an amount of money
10.	○	○	a product or service

C7 **My grandmother** *(sich) erinnern, Gedächtnis, Erinnerung*

Ergänzen Sie.

My grandmother says that her (1.) m _ m _ _ y is failing.
Like a lot of older people she can (2.) r _ _ _ _ _ _ _ many things from a long time ago, and some of her (3.) m _ _ _ _ _ _ _ are really vivid. But she has problems with her (4.) s _ _ _ _-term m _ _ _ _ _. She goes into the garden, for example, and then can't (5.) r _ _ _ _ _ _ _ what she went for. And she forgets things like doctor's appointments. She needs someone or something to (6.) r _ _ _ _ _ her.
For her last birthday we grandchildren gave her a mobile phone and showed her how to use the organizer function, so that she gets a (7.) r _ _ _ _ _ _ _ when she needs one. But of course she only gets it if she (8.) r _ _ _ _ _ _ _ _ to switch the mobile on!

C8 A crossword *gesund*

Ergänzen Sie.

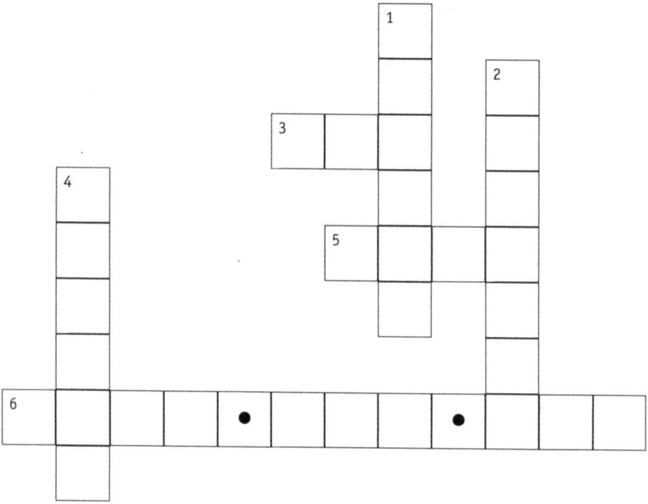

Across

3. My grandmother is still f_ _ and well at the age of 96.
5. I was sorry to hear that you're in hospital. Get w_ _ _ soon!
6. At least there's one thing that the experts seem to agree on – that fruit and vegetables are g_ _ _ f_ _ y_ _.

Down

1. Dave was ill last week, but he's b_ _ _ _ _ again now and back at work.
2. The older you get, the more important it is to adopt a h_ _ _ _ _ _ lifestyle.
4. If you use your c_ _ _ _ _ sense, it's obvious what you should do.

C9 More coming and going *fahren*

Welche Form ist richtig?

1. The traffic got so bad that I gave up ... to work. I now commute by train.
   a. going
   b. driving
   c. travelling
2. Is it difficult to ... a heavy motorbike?
   a. drive b. lead
   c. ride
3. Now that the high-speed line has been completed, trains ... at over 250 km/h and the journey time has been almost halved.
   a. drive
   b. ride
   c. travel
4. How often do the trains ... at this time of day?
   a. ride b. drive
   c. run
5. It's OK, I'm going your way. I'll ... .
   a. drive you home
   b. travel you home
   c. bring you home
6. In the evenings I usually ... .
   a. go with the 6 o'clock train
   b. take the 6 o'clock train
   c. ride the 6 o'clock train
7. It was late so we ... .
   a. went home with a taxi
   b. took a taxi home
   c. drove home with a taxi
8. There was a police radar trap, but I was OK. I was only ... a little over 50 km/h.
   a. doing
   b. driving
   c. riding
9. If it's wet, I don't walk but ... .
   a. go with the bus
   b. take the bus
   c. ride the bus to work
10. How fast does this moped ...?
    a. drive b. go c. do
11. I ... when I was 17.
    a. learned to drive
    b. made my driving
    c. did my driving licence

C10 **People who teach** *Lehrer*

Ergänzen Sie *teacher* oder *instructor*.

1. a driving ____________________

2. a school ____________________

3. a riding ____________________

4. a swimming ________________

5. a university ________, or lecturer
6. People who teach skills are called __________s.
7. People who teach a school or academic subject are called __________s.

C11 **Not much room** *eng*

Ergänzen Sie eine passende Übersetzung von „eng".

close • closely • narrow • tight

1. These trousers are __________. Have they shrunk in the wash, or have I put on weight?
2. We've been __________ friends for over 10 years.
3. Be careful, at the bottom of the hill is a __________ bend.
4. The words *thanks* and *danke* are __________ related.

12 The right preposition *gegen*

Ergänzen Sie eine passende Entsprechung für „gegen".

1. Es tut mir leid, aber ich kann nichts „dagegen" tun.
   I'm very sorry, but I can't do anything ________ it.
2. Nehmen Sie etwas gegen Ihren Heuschnupfen?
   Are you taking anything ________ your hay fever?
3. Wir müssten irgendwann gegen 10 ankommen.
   We should arrive sometime ________ 10.
4. Die Mannschaft hat gegen eine viel schwächere verloren.
   The team lost ________ a much weaker one.
5. Es hat viel Widerstand gegen den Plan gegeben.
   There has been a lot of resistance ________ the plan.
6. Er war zu schnell und ist gegen eine Mauer gefahren.
   He was too fast and drove ________ a wall.
7. Die Geiseln wurden gegen Gefangene ausgetauscht.
   The hostages were exchanged ________ prisoners.

13 A play *spielen*

Wählen Sie die richtige Lösung, a oder b.

I can't (a.) act / (b.) play theatre (1.), but I enjoy going to the theatre. Our local theatre recently (a.) performed / (b.) played (2.) a comedy that (a.) was set / (b.) played (3.) in the 1980s. Somebody I know (a.) acted / (b.) played (4.) the lead. He (a.) acted / (b.) played (5.) a footballer who loves scoring own goals.

1	2	3	4	5

C14 Big, tall, great? *groß*

Ergänzen Sie.

big • great • large • tall

1. Jem's over 1 metre 90 __________.
2. Will it make a __________ difference?
3. I have __________ respect for her.
4. It was a __________ mistake to invite Adrian.
5. They paid a very __________ amount.
6. Personal coaching is __________ business these days.
7. Was Clinton a __________ president?
8. Fiona is my __________ sister. She's two years older.
9. It was a moment of __________ danger.
10. Who lives in that __________ house at the end of the road?
11. She's almost forgotten now, but 20 years ago she was a __________ star.
12. He was a good teacher. He had __________ patience and understanding.

C15 Small or little? *klein*

Ergänzen Sie *small* oder *little.*

1. Which number is __________er: 2.75 or 2?
2. She's just given birth to a __________ boy.
3. They live in a lovely __________ village on the lakeside.
4. The password is 'admin', all in __________ letters.
5. You only need a __________ amount of sugar.
6. Do you have any __________ change, for the parking meter?
7. The room was a bit __________, but it was OK for one night.
8. A __________ car uses less petrol.
9. Our ex-boss was a nasty __________ man.
10. Joey is my __________ brother. I'm a year older than him.

C16 What was that? *verstehen*

Was ist richtig: a oder b?

1. Could you speak a bit louder, please. At the back of the room here we can't (a.) hear / (b.) understand what you're saying.

2. The article was about molecules and sub-atomic particles. I'm not a scientist and I couldn't (a.) hear / (b.) understand what it was all about.

3. Can you hold on a minute while I just shut my door. There's a group of visitors being shown round and there's so much noise that I can't (a.) hear / (b.) understand you properly.

1	2	3

C17 A crossword *bleiben*

Ergänzen Sie.

Across

1. How long do you want to _ _ _ _? One night or two?
3. Little _ _ _ _ _ _ _ _ to be done. Most things are now under control.
4. What's the time? This clock seems to have _ _ _ _ _ _ _ _.

Down

1. We all remained _ _ _ _ _ _ _ _ _ _ until the guest of honour sat down.
2. Please _ _ _ _ quiet, or you'll frighten it away.

C18 A question of speed *schnell*

Ergänzen Sie *fast* oder *quick(ly)*.

1. The car wasn't driving very __________ .
2. I'll just have a __________ look at the sales figures.
3. It's a good __________ road with little traffic.
4. We've got time for a __________ cup of coffee.
5. Wilson ran one of the __________est races of her career.
6. Can you tell me __________ what I'll need to take with me?

C19 Places *Platz*

Welcher Ausdruck ist richtig?

1. Can you make ... for one more?
   ○ place ○ room
2. In the centre of town there is a big ... .
   ○ place ○ square
3. Excuse me, ...? – Sorry. Someone's sitting there.
   ○ is this place free ○ is this seat taken
4. The hotel has two tennis ... .
   ○ courts ○ places ○ pitches
5. It also has a golf ... .
   ○ course ○ court ○ place
6. The school sold its ... for redevelopment, to raise money.
   ○ sport field ○ sport place ○ sports ground
7. Janice has got a ... at one of the elite universities.
   ○ place ○ study place ○ studying place
8. Come in and ... .
   ○ have a seat ○ take place
9. Down by the river would be a good ... to have our barbecue party.
   ○ place ○ space
10. There's ... for the rest of the books in this box here.
    ○ place ○ room

C20 Getting from A to B *Reise, Fahrt*

Was passt in die Lücke? Mehrere Lösungen sind möglich.

1.
- ◆ We weren't expecting you this early.
- ● Yes, it was a very easy ... today, there was very little traffic on the road.

  ○ drive ○ journey ○ trip

2.
- ◆ Do you think you could look after our dog one weekend?
- ● Sure. You want to go away?
- ◆ Yes, we'd like to go on a ... to Amsterdam.

  ○ weekend travel ○ weekend trip ○ weekend journey

3.
- ◆ How far are you from the centre of town?
- ● Just a ... .

  ○ ten-minute bus ride ○ journey of ten minutes with the bus ○ short drive by bus

4.
- ◆ Would you describe ... as one of your hobbies?
- ● It would be if I could afford to get away more often!

  ○ travels ○ travel ○ journeying

5.
- ◆ Have you been to Bulgaria before?
- ● No. We've booked a ten-day guided ... so that we can get a feel for the country.

  ○ journey ○ trip ○ tour

6.
- ◆ We need to cut down on our outgoings[1].
- ● Well, one way would be to reduce the number of ... we make.

  ○ car travels ○ car drives ○ car journeys

[1]Ausgaben

C21 How long (1)? *brauchen*

Drücken Sie den Sachverhalt besser aus – benutzen Sie *take*.

◆ How long ~~do I need~~ from here to Strasbourg?
1. ______________________________
● ~~You need~~ about four hours by car.
2. ______________________________

◆ ~~I needed~~ two whole days to get my presentation ready.
3. ______________________________
● I know. That sort of thing ~~needs~~ a lot of time.
4. ______________________________

C22 How long (2)? *dauern, brauchen*

Übersetzen Sie.

1. Ich brauche deine Hilfe. Es dauert nur ein paar Minuten.

   ____

2. Du brauchst nicht auf mich zu warten.

   ____

3. Mit dem Zug braucht man anderthalb Stunden.

   ____

4. Die Reise dauert anderthalb Stunden.

   ____

5. Der Film dauert 30 Minuten.

   ____

6. Sie brauchen nichts mitzubringen, wir haben alles.

   ____

7. Ich brauche noch zwei Stunden. Für diese Art von Arbeit braucht man lange.

   ____

C23 Will it hold? *halten*

Was ist richtig: a oder b? Oder sind a und b beide richtig?

1. Will the fine weather (a.) keep / (b.) hold till the weekend?
2. (a.) Hold / (b.) Stop the thief!
3. The crisis (a.) held on / (b.) lasted for well over a year.
4. What's that (a.) you're holding / (b.) you're keeping in your hand? Can I see?
5. We always (a.) held him for trustworthy/ (b.) thought of him as trustworthy.
6. I was so tired, I could hardly (a.) hold / (b.) keep my eyes open.
7. The eggs will (a.) hold / (b.) keep longer in the fridge of course.
8. I need some light. Can you (a.) hold / (b.) keep the torch for me while I try and see what's wrong?
9. Which driver (a.) holds / (b.) keeps the record for the Monza circuit?
10. If you want to be trusted, you have to (a.) hold to / (b.) stick to the rules.
11. I don't trust them. They never (a.) hold / (b.) keep their promise.
12. Just (a.) hold to / (b.) keep to the left and you'll be OK.
13. I mustn't (a.) hold you / (b.) keep you. I expect you have lots to do.
14. To mark the occasion, the vice-president (a.) held / (b.) made a short speech.
15. The friendship didn't (a.) hold / (b.) last long.
16. Can you (a.) hold / (b.) keep your breath for a minute? Try it.

1	2	3	4	5	6	7	8

9	10	11	12	13	14	15	16

C24 How about Wednesday? *passen*

Ergänzen Sie.

fit • match • suit

1. How about Wednesday? Does that _______ you?
2. I always used to think that green didn't _______ me.
3. If the text doesn't _______, you can take this paragraph out.
4. This unit is not quite so wide and should _______ in the corner quite nicely.
5. You can't wear that jacket with those trousers. They don't _______.

C25 What's your son doing? *Studium, studieren*

Was passt in die Lücke? Mehrere Lösungen sind möglich.

1. What's your son doing now? – He ...
   a. is a student c. is at university
   b. studies economics d. studies
2. A lot of top managers in fact never ...
   a. studyed c. were on the university
   b. did a study d. went to university
3. A lot of ... in Britain last not more than three years.
   a. courses c. degree courses
   b. studies d. university courses
4. When are you going to ... ?
   a. begin your study c. start university
   b. begin the studies d. start the university
5. What ... has she chosen?
   a. course c. study
   b. subject d. study course
6. Do many students in this country have jobs ...?
   a. during the study c. when they are at studies
   b. during studies d. when they're at university

1	2	3	4	5	6

C26 By or not by? *bei*

Korrigieren Sie.

1. We didn't stay in a hotel. We stayed ~~by~~ _______ friends.
2. I'm staying ~~by~~ _______ Leonard's place. He has a spare room.
3. ~~By~~ _______ so many problems, it's difficult to know where to start.
4. We live ~~by~~ _______ Hamburg.
5. I work ~~by~~ _______ a firm in the textile industry.
6. She met her partner ~~by~~ _______ a seminar.
7. Let's discuss this in peace and quiet ~~by~~ _______ a glass of wine.
8. People say the view is best ~~by~~ _______ sunset.
9. He died ~~by~~ _______ a car accident.
10. I'm afraid I only have € 20 ~~by~~ _______ me.
11. Guess who I met ~~by~~ _______ the baker's this morning.
12. I stood and watched her ~~by~~ _______ her work.
13. It was not very comfortable ~~by~~ _______ the temperature around zero.

C27 On the job *Arbeit*

Ergänzen Sie *work* oder *job*.

◆ What's your (1.) __________?

● I'm a photographer.

◆ That sounds like interesting (2.) __________.

● That's what most people think, but it's actually quite hard (3.) __________, with a lot of stress if you want to make money at it. It's certainly not my dream (4.) __________.

◆ OK.

● I'm hoping to change my (5.) __________. What I'd really like is a (6.) __________ with animals.

C28 A changed man *(an)erkennen*

Ergänzen Sie *realized* oder *recognized*.

1. He'd lost so much weight that I hardly __________ him.
2. Few people __________ how serious the problem was.
3. I suddenly __________ that I had no money on me.
4. Nobody __________ what had happened till it was too late.
5. Several governments have already __________ the new regime.

C29 **A crossword** *endlich, schließlich*

Ergänzen Sie.

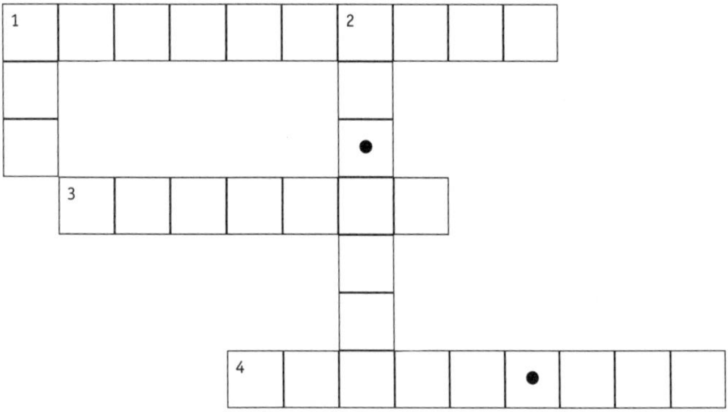

Across

1. It was a long search, but e _ _ _ _ _ _ _ _ _ y we found what we were looking for.
3. It's f _ _ _ _ _ y stopped raining!
4. You can't expect too much of him, a _ _ _ _ a _ _ he's still only 14.

Down

1. I made several offers to help, but he didn't respond, so in the _ _ _ I just left him to it.
2. We've paid off all our debts, a _ l _ _ _!

C30 A question of weight *leicht*

Wählen Sie die richtige Lösung.

1. This bag is so ... . It feels as though it's empty.
   ● easy ● light ● slight
2. I'm afraid we seem to have a ... problem.
   ● easy ● light ● slight
3. The exam was actually quite ... .
   ● easy ● light ● slight
4. There has been ... improvement in the economic situation.
   ● an easy ● a light ● a slight
5. ... wind was blowing from the northeast.
   ● An easy ● A light ● A slight
6. There was only one really acceptable offer, so ... to decide which to accept.
   ● I found it easy ● It fell easy ● It was a slight question

C31 Not from *von*

Korrigieren Sie.

1. It's one of many films ~~from~~ Steven Spielberg.
   ____
2. Oxford is northwest ~~from~~ London.
   ____
3. Six ~~from~~ ten people think the government has handled the crisis well.
   ____
4. Jason is a friend ~~from me~~ from my schooldays.
   ____
5. This magazine article is ~~from~~ someone I know.
   ____
6. The shop is in the arcade to the right ~~from~~ the station.
   ____

C32 More weight *schwer*

Was passt in die Lücke? Mehrere Lösungen sind möglich.

1. How ... is your hand luggage?
   a. great b. serious c. heavy
2. I'm ... disappointed.
   a. deeply b. heavily c. greatly
3. It's ... to imagine what the world would be like without it.
   a. heavy b. hard c. difficult
4. I'm not really ill. It's just a ... cold.
   a. heavy b. great c. deep
5. You have to be ... to own property in Monte Carlo.
   a. heavily rich b. violently rich c. stinking rich
6. Some of the questions were easy, but a few were really ... .
   a. heavy b. serious c. difficult
7. Fortunately, they've not been ... injured.
   a. heavily b. seriously c. badly
8. ... fighting continues in the area controlled by the rebels.
   a. heavy b. hard c. big
9. People like that deserve to be ... punished.
   a. seriously b. deeply c. severely
10. I realize now that it was a ... mistake.
    a. heavy b. serious c. big
11. Old people are often ... .
    a. heavy in hearing b. hard of hearing c. heavy hearing
12. The storm caused ... damage.
    a. grave b. serious c. severe

C33 Bad and worse (1) *schlecht*

Wählen Sie die passende Übersetzung.

1.
◆ Let's see if we can find a suitable time. How about Wednesday?
● *Mittwoch ist schlecht.* Could we make it Thursday instead?

a. Wednesday is bad.
b. Wednesday is difficult.
c. Wednesday is poor.

2.
◆ How long do you think we'll need?
● *Das kann ich schlecht sagen.* Two hours, three hours, something like that.

a. I cannot say that well.
b. I cannot really tell it.
c. I cannot really say.

3.
◆ What shall we tell him – if he asks?
● *Wir können ihm schlecht sagen, dass wir ihm nicht vertrauen.*

a. We can hardly tell him that we don't trust him.
b. We can't well tell him that we don't trust him.
c. We can badly say that we don't trust him.

4.
◆ It's cold in here.
● Yes, I'm sorry. It's this window. *Es schließt schlecht.*

a. It shuts badly.
b. It doesn't shut well.
c. It doesn't shut properly.

1	2	3	4

C34 Bad and worse (2) *schlecht*

Ergänzen Sie. Verwenden Sie jedes Wort nur einmal.

bad • sick • off • poor • poorly

1. Business is not just _________, it's terrible at present.
2. Gone are the days when Chinese products were good value for money but rather _________ quality.
3. I don't like the look or the smell of this fish. I think it's _________.
4. What's the matter, Jack? You don't look very well. – I feel _________.
5. The meeting was _________ attended: only six people came.

C35 All & every *alle(s)*

Übersetzen Sie.

1. Alle denken das Gleiche.
   ____
2. Ich bin bereit alles [egal was] zu tun, um dir zu helfen.
   ____
3. Alle zwei oder drei Tage bekomme ich eine E-Mail.
   ____
4. Mein Motto ist: Alles oder nichts.
   ____
5. Wir brauchen alle eine Pause.
   ____
6. Alle Leute waren begeistert.
   ____

C36 Dates and deadlines *bis*

Was ist richtig: a oder b?

1. I'll wait (a.) till / (b.) to six.
2. If they haven't arrived (a.) till / (b.) by then, I'll go without them.
3. You'll have the data (a.) by / (b.) until the end of the week, I promise.
4. There must have been (a.) till / (b.) up to 100 people there.
5. In the holidays they often sleep (a.) till / (b.) to at least 11.
6. (a.) By the time / (b.) Until we'd finished, it was dark.
7. I should get home (a.) till / (b.) by about 7.30, but it might be later.
8. I can count (a.) till / (b.) up to ten in Arabic.
9. Walk along here (a.) till / (b.) as far as the Imperial Hotel.
10. The artist covered the building in silver foil from top (a.) till / (b.) to bottom.

1	2	3	4	5	6	7	8	9	10

C37 Twins *gleich*

Ergänzen Sie Angaben (1.) zum Alter, (2.) zur Größe und (3.) zur Kleidung.

David and Peter are twins. As twins, they are of course

(1.) ____________________. But they are also
(2.) ____________________, and they often wear
(3.) ____________________.

C38 A waiter's questions *fertig*

Was fragt der Kellner? Verwenden Sie einmal *ready*, einmal *finished*.

C39 A question of ability *können*

Ordnen Sie zu und ergänzen Sie die rechte Spalte.

1. Ich kann kein Spanisch.
2. Du kannst es wirklich gut!
3. Das kann ja jeder.
4. Wir können gut mit einander.
5. Wie konnten Sie nur?!
6. Ich kann einfach nicht mehr.

a. You're really good _______ it.
b. We _______ _______ well together.
c. I don't _______ Spanish.
d. I just can't _______ on.
e. Anyone can _______ that!
f. How _______ you?!

1	2	3	4	5	6

C40 Change *werden*

Welcher Ausdruck ist richtig? Oder sind beide richtig?

1. Bonnie says she wants to ... a journalist when she grows up.
   ○ be ○ become
2. I'll ... mad if I get any more email enquiries like this.
   ○ become ○ go
3. It's autumn, and the leaves ... yellow, brown and red.
   ○ are turning ○ become
4. It ... very difficult to find new markets for our products.
   ○ is becoming ○ is getting
5. As I ... old, there are many things I no longer take so seriously.
   ○ go ○ grow
6. They were forecasting rain, but the weather ... better than expected.
   ○ has got ○ has turned out
7. When I heard Giorgio was coming, I ... very excited.
   ○ got ○ went
8. My hair ... grey, and it makes me feel old.
   ○ is going ○ becomes

C41 Oh *(be)merken, sich merken*

Ergänzen Sie. Verwenden Sie jedes Wort nur einmal.

note • notice • realize

1. I'm sorry. I didn't ________ you'd already arrived. The message didn't reach me. Have you been waiting long?
2. Please ________ that there are certain things you're no longer allowed to take in your hand baggage.
3. I ________d that there was a small crowd of people, but at the time I didn't think anything about it.

C42 **Time** *Zeit*

Korrigieren Sie.

1. I haven't seen Raymond much ~~in the last time.~~

   ____

2. ~~In the first time,~~ when I was new to the job, there was a lot to learn.

   ____

3. I'm going to be travelling quite a lot ~~in the next time.~~

   ____

C43 **Once & more** *einmal*

Übersetzen Sie. Verwenden Sie die angegebenen Ausdrücke.

1. Sind Sie schon einmal in Mexiko gewesen? *(ever)*

   ____

2 Ich war schon einmal in New York. *(before)*

   ____

3. Ich würde gern einmal Irland besuchen. *(sometime)*

   ____

4. Hören Sie gut zu, denn ich sage es nur einmal. *(once)*

   ____

5. Es war einmal ein König ... *(once upon a time)*

   ____

6. Die Stadt war einmal berühmt. *(once)*

   ____

C44 In the past *früher, frühere(r/s)*
Welcher Ausdruck ist richtig?

1. It's her second marriage. Her ... was called Heinz, too.
   - earlier husband
   - ex-husband
   - husband before
2. They each have a son from ... .
   - an ex-marriage
   - a previous marriage
   - a marriage before
3. We ... in Hamburg.
   - lived earlier
   - former lived
   - used to live
4. I apologize for my lateness. I couldn't make it any ... .
   - more earlier
   - more previously
   - sooner
5. It was ... a nice place to live, but all this new development has spoiled it.
   - earlier
   - once
   - sooner
6. For sale. Only one ... owner.
   - earlier
   - former
   - previous
7. I was born and grew up in the ... East Germany.
   - earlier
   - former
   - previous
8. He says he won't be able to attend 'because of ... engagement'.
   - an earlier
   - a former
   - a previous
9. The place was ... quite famous.
   - earlier
   - once
   - earlier once
10. We ... quite often.
    - used to meet
    - met earlier
    - met previously

C45 A question of position *stehen*
Ergänzen Sie die Übersetzung.

1. Tut mir leid, er steht unter der Dusche.
   Sorry, ______________ a shower.

2. In der Zeitung steht, dass Monkton gewonnen hat.
   In the paper ______________ that Monkton has won.

3. Gelb steht dir.
   Yellow ______________ you.

4. Der Zug war voll und ich musste stehen.
   The train was full and I had to ______________ .

5. Der Rettungsplan steht jetzt.
   The rescue plan ______________ .

C46 While or during? *während*
Wählen Sie die richtige Lösung.

(a.) During / (b.) While (1.) students, James and I had weekend and evening jobs at the same restaurant for several months. He worked in the kitchen, (a.) during / (b.) while (2.) I served out front. We worked there for (a.) during / (b.) while (3.) the summer holidays, too. It was hard, I remember, because we didn't have a single day off (a.) while the whole eight weeks / (b.) throughout the whole eight weeks (4.).

1	2	3	4

C47 Power *stark*

Welcher Ausdruck passt in die Lücke?

1. There is a ... westerly wind.

   ● heavy ● powerful ● strong

2. He was once a ... smoker.

   ● strong ● heavy ● great

3. It's been raining ... all morning.

   ● strongly ● heavily ● violently

4. Expect another ... frost tonight.

   ● powerful ● hard ● strong

5. Fortunately she's not in ... pain.

   ● great ● heavy ● strong

6. There's ... traffic on all roads out of the capital.

   ● strong ● heavy ● hard

7. The roof has been ... damaged.

   ● strongly ● hard ● badly

8. I'm afraid I have ... reservations[1] about the plan.

   ● strong ● grand ● violent

9. We are ... dependent on what happens in the global economy.

   ● strongly ● heavily ● much

10. She published her memoirs in a ... book.

    ● 600-page long ● 600-page strong heavy ● 600-page

[1]Vorbehalte, Zweifel

C48 A crossword *vor*

Ergänzen Sie.

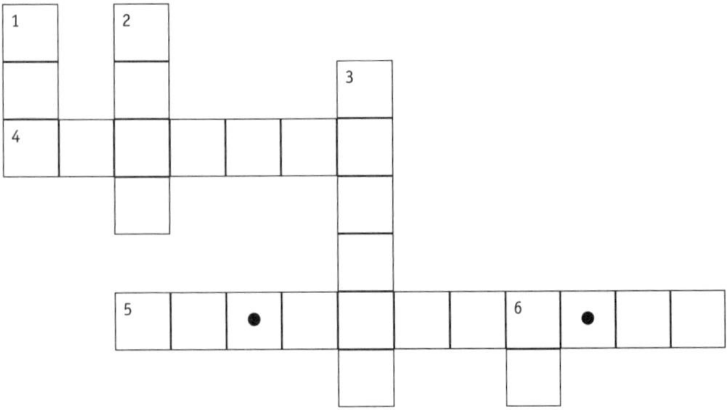

Across
4. I'll meet you o _ _ _ _ _ _ _ the main entrance.
5. You can't park i _ f _ _ _ _ _ o _ the building, only at the back.

Down
1. I spoke to him only ten minutes _ _ _.
2. He was trembling[1] w _ _ _ fear.
3. I'll try and be there b _ _ _ _ _ _ the others.
6. It's two minutes _ _ two.

[1]zitterte

C49 Not busy *ruhig*
Ergänzen Sie.

calm • quiet • still

1. We live in a _________ street in the suburbs.
2. She always seems to have everything under control and remains _________ in the wildest chaos.
3. The wind was light, the sea was nice and _________.
4. Is something troubling you? You're so _________. You've not said anything all evening.
5. If you won't sit _________, how am I supposed to put the plaster on?

C50 How? *wie*
Übersetzen Sie.

1. Wie läuft es? Alles in Ordnung?
   ____
2. Wie war das Wetter?
   ____
3. Wie ist der neue Chef?
   ____
4. Wie sagt man das auf Englisch?
   ____
5. Wie nennt man dieses Ding auf Englisch?
   ____
6. Wie ist die Telefonnummer?
   ____
7. Wie war es, allein zu reisen?
   ____
8. Es ist ein Gebäude wie ein Hotel.
   ____
9. Er ist nicht so alt wie sie.
   ____
10. Wir haben ihm vertraut, wie viele Menschen es taten.
   ____

C51 With us or against us? *auch*

Welcher Ausdruck passt in die Lücke?

1. Wallis is normally against this sort of idea, but ... he seems to be in favour.

   also / even / too

2. I need a break. – ... .

   I also / Me too / I as well

3. I like the design. – ... .

   I also / So do I / So do I too

4. We won't arrive till quite late. – ... .

   Neither will we / Nor we / We also not

5. I'm afraid I haven't understood this. – You're not the only one. I don't understand it ... .

   too / either / nor

6. ... it costs more, I think this is the better solution.

   Also if / Even if / Even when

7. The roof has been damaged and ... have two windows.

   also / even / so

C52 I know *bewusst*
Ergänzen Sie *aware* oder *conscious*.

1. I'm very ____________ that this is not an easy decision for you.
2. As far as I'm ____________, no other company has a comparable product.
3. I didn't ____________ly try to take advantage of the situation.
4. It was not a very ____________ decision on my part.
5. People nowadays are very energy-____________, partly because of the cost of energy, partly for environmental reasons.

C53 Permission to drive *Führerschein*
Übersetzen Sie.

1. Die Polizei wollte meinen Führerschein sehen.

   ____

2. Unser Sohn hat gerade angefangen, den Führerschein zu machen.

   ____

3. Unsere Tochter hat bereits den Führerschein.

   ____

C54 Having things with you *tragen*

Ergänzen Sie.

bear • carry • support • wear

1. How formal is this event? What should I ______________?
2. That looks heavy. I'll help you ______________ it.
3. The platform is ______________ed by one central pillar[1].
4. You should ______________ some sort of ID with you at all times.
5. It's a terrible responsibility for her to have to ______________ on her own.
6. Let's hope all this hard work eventually ______________s fruit.
7. I don't normally ______________ a watch at the weekend. My life is so governed by the clock during the week.
8. Who is going to ______________ the costs – us or them?
9. Didn't you use to ______________ glasses?

[1]Säule

C55 Up there *über*

Was passt in die Lücke? Mehrere Lösungen sind möglich.

1. Jackson's office is on the floor ... us.	a. above b. over
2. Andy was in the class ... me at school.	a. above b. over
3. She's always complaining ... the food.	a. about b. on c. over
4. I'm travelling ... Frankfurt because the flight's cheaper.	a. by the way of b. over c. via
5. It can only be a few degrees ... freezing this morning.	a. above b. over c. up of
6. Results this year were well ... average.	a. above b. beyond c. over
7. It took her two years to get ... his death.	a. above b. beyond c. over
8. He's the sort of person who laughs ... his own jokes.	a. above b. at c. over
9. The city is about 600 metres ... sea level.	a. above b. beyond c. over
10. Tears ran ... his face.	a. about b. down c. over
11. Is there any money ...?	a. left b. over c. resting
12. We'll be at home ... Christmas this year.	a. at b. during c. over
13. There's no reason to get annoyed ... it.	a. above b. about c. over
14. Her books are famous ... the borders of Wyoming.	a. above b. beyond c. over
15. They sent a bill ... €60,000.	a. over above b. for over c. over more than

C56 Already and more *schon*

Muss der Ausdruck mit „schon" übersetzt werden – ja oder nein?

1. Es ist *schon* ganz schön schwierig sich zu entscheiden.
2. Wir haben *schon* halb drei.
3. Was macht es *schon* für einen Unterschied?
4. Hat Tony *schon* angerufen?
5. *Schon bevor* er aufstand, wusste ich, was er sagen würde.
6. Ich sehe *schon*, dass wir mehr Zeit benötigen.
7. Sind Sie *schon mal* in Disneyland gewesen?
8. Die ersten Gäste sind *schon* da.
9. Was weiß *er* mit 18 *schon* vom Leben?
10. *Schon bald* werden wir die ersten Ergebnisse wissen.

Übersetzen Sie die Sätze, in denen „schon" mit übersetzt werden muss.

____

____

____

____

____

____

D. Confusing friends

Englische Wortpaare mit ähnlicher Form aber unterschiedlicher Bedeutung

D1 advice / advise
Ergänzen Sie.

◆ Do you have a moment?
● Sure.
◆ I'd like to ask your (1.) __________.
● What about?
◆ Well, can you (2.) __________ me what to do in a case like this? You see, ...

D2 homework / housework
Ordnen Sie zu.

1. Exercises and tasks given by a teacher	a. housework
2. Cleaning, cooking, etc.	b. homework

D3 interesting / interested
Wählen Sie die richtige Lösung.

◆ There's a photo exhibition next week about the Sahara. Are you (a.) interested / (b.) interesting (1.)? Would you like to go?
● It certainly sounds (a.) interested / (b.) interesting (2.). I've always (a.) been interested in / (b.) been interested for (3.) Africa.

1	2	3

D4 desert / dessert

Übersetzen Sie.

1. Ist die Sahara die größte Wüste der Erde?

   ____

2. Was möchten Sie als Nachspeise?

   ____

D5 economic / economical

Ergänzen Sie.

1. The __________ situation is improving.
2. The government's __________ policies have been successful.
3. The new models are much more __________ and use an average of 15% less energy.
4. It's not a good idea to start a new business in the present __________ climate.
5. It's much more __________ to buy in bulk[1].
6. It's a brilliant design, so __________ on space.

D6 classic / classical

Korrigieren Sie – falls nötig!

1. I don't listen to much *classic* __________ music.
2. This is a *classic* __________ case of poor communication.
3. I can't understand people who go to university to study *classic* __________ Greek.
4. Spielberg has directed a number of *classic* __________ films.
5. I made the *classic* __________ mistake.
6. She's just as much at home in *classic* __________ theatre as in contemporary plays.

[1]in großen Mengen kaufen

D7 beside / besides

Welcher Ausdruck ist richtig?

1. Come and sit ... me.

   ● beside ● besides

2. Do you know anyone else ... the hosts?

   ● beside ● besides

3. I don't have time, and ..., it costs too much.

   ● beside ● besides

4. I do several other sports ... sailing.

   ● beside ● besides

5. ... full time, I also perform as a cabaret artist.

   ● Besides to work ● Besides working

6. My problems seem so insignificant ... yours.

   ● beside ● besides

D8 it's / its

Ergänzen Sie.

1. ___________ so cold in here!
2. The car has some rust, but ___________ engine is OK.
3. The hospital has ___________ own emergency power supply.
4. Somehow the company seems to have lost ___________ way.
5. ___________ called *The Arena*.
6. Sorry, what's ___________ name?

D9 all together / altogether

Ergänzen Sie.

1.
- ◆ Are you paying separately or together?
- ● Well, how much is it ___________?
- ◆ € 146.80.
- ● OK, together.

2.
- ◆ It seems ages since we last met.
- ● It is, in fact I can't remember the last time we were ___________

D10 lay / lie

Ergänzen Sie die passende Verbform.

1. Jacob's tired. He's just gone to ___________ down for a bit.
2. I hate it when Mr Smithers ___________ his hand on my arm.
3. Just think. All this stuff has ___________ here unnoticed for over 50 years.
4. I'm sorry. I ___________ to you, but it was because I wanted to protect you from the truth.
5. This time last week we were ___________ on the beach with not a care in the world.
6. The new carpets are being ___________ today.
7. What's that ___________ on the floor? It looks like a banknote.
8. Snow ___________ on the ground and it was bitterly cold.

Infinitiv	Vergangenheit	Present Perfect
9. (to) lay (*legen*)	___________	have/has ___________
10. (to) lie (*liegen*)	___________	have/has ___________
11. (to) lie (*lügen*)	___________	have/has ___________

D11 greatly / largely

Kreuzen Sie die richtige Lösung an.

	greatly	largely	
1.	●	●	The forest fires are now ... under control.
2.	●	●	Success is ... a question of who you know.
3.	●	●	Reactions have varied ... .
4.	●	●	Any help would be ... appreciated.

D12 past / passed

Ergänzen Sie.

1. We're on the M3 and have just ___________ exit 12, so we should be with you in about another 20 minutes.
2. We've driven ___________ exit 12.
3. Half an hour ___________ without anything new happening.
4. Has anything happened in the ___________ half hour?
5. It's now ten ___________ four.
6. I thought I just heard someone walk ___________ my door.
7. In the ___________ this place was actually quite famous.
8. But those days have ___________

D13 terrible / terrific

Ordnen Sie zu.

1. We've had a terrific holiday.
2. We've had a terrible holiday.

a. It's been absolutely fabulous.
b. Everything that could go wrong did go wrong.

D14 used to / be/get used to
Welcher Ausdruck passt in die Lücke?

1. I ... for an Italian company before I came here.

   ○ used to work ○ am used to work ○ get used to working

2. When I broke my arm, I suddenly ... with my left hand.

   ○ used to write ○ was used to write ○ had to get used to writing

3. It comes as a shock to most people, but you ... after a while.

   ○ use to it ○ are used it ○ get used to it

4. I ... English in my job. It comes naturally now.

   ○ used to use ○ am used to using ○ am used to use

D15 at last / at least
Ergänzen Sie.

◆ The documentation is complete (1.) _______________.
● How long has it taken to produce it?
◆ I can't remember when we started, but it must be (2.) _______________ six months ago.

D16 raise / rise
Ergänzen Sie die passende Verbform.

1. The price of petrol has _____________ again.
2. They've _____________ prices again.
3. I _____________ my arm to signal that I had a question.
4. Tension _____________ in the room as the discussion intensified.
5. It was mid-winter and the sun _____________ late.
6. We need to _____________ standards.

D17 sometime / sometimes
Was ist richtig: a oder b?

◆ I hope we meet again (a.) sometime / (b.) sometimes (1.).
● Yes, that would be nice.
◆ I (a.) sometime / (b.) sometimes (2.) have to go to Antwerp on business. Maybe we could meet up there?

D18 everyday / every day
Wählen Sie die richtige Lösung.

◆ This sort of thing doesn't happen (a.) every day / (b.) everyday (1.) thank goodness!
● Absolutely! Can you imagine what would happen if this was an (a.) every day / (b.) everyday (2.) occurrence?

D19 historic / historical
Kreuzen Sie die richtige Lösung an.

	historic	historical	
1.	●	●	It was a ... day when peace was declared.
2.	●	●	What you've just told me – is it myth or ... fact?
3.	●	●	People in ... costumes act as guides round the museum.
4.	●	●	Can you explain the ... background to the conflict?

D20 affect / effect
Wählen Sie die richtige Lösung.

◆ What (a.) affect / (b.) effect (1.) are all these changes going to have on us personally, in this department?
● To be honest, I don't think they're going to (a.) affect / (b.) effect (2.) us much at all.

D21 loose / lose
Ergänzen Sie.

1. There was a __________ connection in the plug, that's why the hair dryer wasn't working.
2. Don't __________ it, or we shall be in real trouble!
3. Please don't go. It's dangerous and I don't want to __________ you.
4. It's often cheaper to buy things __________ rather than packaged.

D22 major / mayor
Wer ist was?

1. ______________________ 2. ______________________

D23 in time / on time
Was ist richtig: a oder b?

1. We arrived dead (a.) in / (b.) on time.
2. The train is almost always late, but today, for once, it was (a.) in / (b.) on time.
3. I hope to get there (a.) in / (b.) on time to see the end of the match.

E. All friends together

Gemischte Übungen

E1 In the pub

Korrigieren Sie.

1. ~~I become~~ a Guinness, please.
2. I'd like something to eat, too. Can I see the ~~card~~, please?
3. People say English ~~kitchen~~ is not very good, but I don't believe that.
4. Oh, excuse me. My ~~handy~~ is ringing.
5. This is a really nice old ~~guesthouse.~~ I come here most days on my way home from work.
6. This smoking ban – do you agree with it? What's your ~~meaning?~~

E2 An evening at the theatre

Ergänzen Sie. Wählen Sie aus der folgenden Auswahl.

audience • badly visited • interval • pause
piece • play • poorly attended • public spectator

◆ So how was it? Did you enjoy the (1.) _________?

● Yes, I did. But it was only a very small (2.) _________. And quite a few of those who were there left in the (3.) _________.

◆ I should have come with you. I hate it when the performances are so (4.) _________________.

E3 Television
Korrigieren Sie.

It's difficult to imagine the days when there was no (1.) ~~private~~ ________________ television and there were only two or three state-financed TV (2.) ~~programmes~~ ________________ to choose from. Those were the days when (3.) ~~newsspeakers~~ ________________ never smiled, but read the (4.) ~~newest~~ ________________ news as if they were at a funeral!

E4 Changes at work
Was ist richtig: a oder b?

◆ How long have you been working here?
● (1.) (a.) For / (b.) Since almost ten years. And you?
◆ Only (2.) (a.) for / (b.) since the beginning of the year.
● There have been a lot of changes here (3.) (a.) in the last time / (b.) recently, with a lot of restructuring.
It's been the same throughout the banking (4.) (a.) branch / (b.) business.
The (5.) (a.) economic / (b.) economical climate is quite different from (6.) (a.) a few years ago / (b.) before a few years.

E5 In the canteen
Übersetzen Sie.

◆ Excuse me, there aren't any (1.) *Tabletts* ____________.
● Some more are just coming.
◆ Thanks. And what's on the (2.) *Speiseplan* ____________ today?
● Vegetarian quiche, or chicken, or you can help yourself from the (3.) *Salatbar* ____________.
◆ I'll do that. Salad is (4.) *gesund*____________.
...
Oh, excuse me. Where's the (5.) *Salatsoße* ____________?

E6 Telephoning

Welcher Ausdruck passt in die Lücke?

1. The phone's ringing. If I ... I'll miss my bus. Can you do it, please?
   - answer it
   - go on it
2. What's the ... for France? Is it 0033?
   - pre-number
   - code
3. Do you want to ..., or shall I say you're not here?
   - accept the conversation
   - take the call
4. When you call back, ... Jane Summertown, then you'll be connected straight to me.
   - ask for
   - demand
5. What number do I have to ... for the police in this country?
   - choose
   - dial
6. The line went dead so I ... .
   - hung up
   - laid the phone down

E7 At school

Korrigieren Sie.

I've just had an invitation to a class ~~meeting~~ ______________ (1.) at my old school, but I don't think I'm going to go. It was a ~~gymnasium~~ ______________ (2.) where all the doctors and lawyers and professional people sent their kids. I never felt that I belonged. I was good ~~in~~ ______________ (3.) most subjects, and I got good ~~notes~~ ______________ (4.) when we ~~wrote~~ ______________ (5.) tests, but I was never really happy there. I wasn't ~~mobbed~~ ______________ (6.) or anything like that, but I was certainly glad when I ~~made~~ ______________ (7.) my final exam, left and ~~started my study~~ ______________ (8.).

E8 Back from holiday

Ergänzen Sie die Übersetzung.

1. Wir haben eine Rundreise durch das ganze Land gemacht.
   We ________ a tour through the whole country.

2. Wir haben nicht in Hotels gewohnt.
   We didn't ________ in hotels.

3. Wir haben in einfachen Pensionen übernachtet.
   We overnighted in simple ________.

4. In Zimmern mit Warm- und Kaltwasser.
   In rooms with ________ and cold water.

5. Die Reise dorthin hat lange gedauert.
   The journey there ________ a long time.

6. Wir haben lange gebraucht.
   ________ ________ ________ a long time.

7. Unsere Pässe wurden ziemlich oft kontrolliert.
   Our passports were ________ quite often.

8. Und wir mussten ständig Formulare ausfüllen.
   And we constantly had to fill in ________.

9. Insgesamt war es eine tolle Reise.
   ________ it was a great trip.

E9 At the weekend

Welcher Ausdruck ist richtig?

1. A lot of people like to ... at the weekend, but that's not my thing.
   - sleep in
   - sleep out
2. Often I go out for a ... on my motorbike.
   - drive
   - ride
3. I ... only a car.
   - used to drive
   - used to driving
4. But ... I sold the car and bought this motorbike.
   - before two years
   - two years ago
5. I ... my driving test for it a couple of months later.
   - made
   - took
6. The test wasn't very ... .
   - hard
   - heavy
7. But I'm not on the ... all the time.
   - road
   - street
8. I also like to be out and about, in ... .
   - the free nature
   - the open air
9. I quite often go ... in the mountains, especially in the autumn.
   - hiking
   - wandering
10. Usually with my camera, because I'm a bit of an amateur ... .
    - photograph
    - photographer
11. I ... the cinema.
    - am also interested in
    - also have interest for
12. You name any ... Hollywood film, I've seen it.
    - classic
    - classical
13. My favourites are ones that ... the first half of the 20th century.
    - are set in
    - play in

E10 Expressions of time

Korrigieren Sie.

Meeting an old friend

◆ You're looking a bit tired.

● Well, I've been under quite a lot of stress (1.) ~~in the last time~~ _______________. You see, I started a new job (2.) ~~a quarter year~~ _______________ ago.

In the office

◆ What's the (3.) ~~newest~~ _______________ news on the joint venture in China?

● (4.) ~~In this stadium~~ _______________ of the project a lot of things are still unclear.

On the radio

◆ It's three minutes past eleven, and here's Steve Mapleton with up-to-date news and information on the (5.) ~~actual~~ _______________ traffic situation.

In a meeting

◆ I suggest we discuss this later, perhaps (6.) ~~while~~ _______________ lunch.

● Yes, it's going to (7.) ~~cost~~ _______________ too much time to do it now.

At tourist information

◆ There's a shuttle bus, or you can walk.

● How long (8.) ~~do you need~~ _______________ to walk?

◆ Not more (9.) ~~as~~ _______________ fifteen mintes.

E11 People

Übersetzen Sie.

1. Ronaldos Frau ist mir sehr sympathisch.

 ____

2. Anna ist sehr selbstbewusst.

 ____

3. Mark ist mein Sohn aus früherer Ehe.

 ____

4. Ich bin gleich alt wie mein Chef.

 ____

5. Sei vorsichtig. Er ist sehr sensibel.

 ____

6. Bitte lass mich in Ruhe! Ich muss arbeiten.

 ____

7. Mein Reitlehrer ist sehr groß, fast zwei Meter groß.

 ____

8. Sei vernünftig!

 ____

9. Warum sind Sie heute so ruhig?

 ____

10. Wann waren wir das letzte Mal alle zusammen?

 ____

11. Mein Mann ist einer der wenigen Männer, die sich nicht für Fußball interessieren.

 ____

12. Die Kinder waren ganz brav.

 ____

E12 A question of health

Welcher Ausdruck ist richtig?

1. Thank you for calling the Exbridge Health Centre. ... are Monday to Friday, 9 to 12.30, and 3 to 6.30.

   ● Consult times ● Speaking times ● Surgery hours

2. They say fruit and vegetables are ..., but only of course if they aren't full of pesticides and things.

   ● good for you ● healthy for you ● good for health

3. The doctor gave me a ... for some pills.

   ● recipe ● prescription ● receipt

4. They gave me some ... for the first few days after the operation.

   ● pain medicine ● pain tablets ● painkillers

5. Grandpa can't find his ... .

   ● false teeth ● replacement teeth ● third teeth

6. You're going to have to take over the presentation. I have ..., I can hardly speak.

   ● a really bad sore throat ● really strong throat pains

   ● really bad throat pains

E13 Tricky pairs

Ergänzen Sie.

nearest, next

1. The train is now approaching Aldringham. Aldringham is the __________ station stop.
2. Where's the __________ station to the hotel?

shade, shadow

3. It's too hot in the sun for me, I'm going to have to move into the __________.
4. I left the autobahn, stopped by a field and had a lie-down in the __________ of a big old oak tree.

back, backside

5. For goodness sake, get up off your __________ and do some work!
6. There are parking spaces at the __________ of the building.

E14 Food & drink

Korrigieren Sie.

1. You can't grow much on a balcony this size, just a few tomatoes, herbs and a couple of ~~salad~~ _________ plants.
2. The fish is served with ~~salt potatoes~~ _________ and a green salad.
3. This curry is ~~sharp~~ _________! How much chili powder did you put in it?
4. The quality of our ~~drink water~~ _________ is actually very good.
5. I need a ~~tablet~~ _________ to carry all these glasses.
6. ~~Good appetite~~ _________ everyone!
7. I'm trying to lose weight and cut down on any food that ~~makes fat~~ ____________.
8. We're planning to ~~grill~~ _________ this evening in the back yard. Why don't you join us?
9. I think it's true that you feel better if you have one ~~warm~~ _________ meal a day.
10. What shall I do with the ~~rests~~ _________ from lunch? Feed them to the dog?
11. We don't eat much bread. If we buy a big ~~bread~~ _________ we often end up throwing half of it away because it's gone stale.
12. Ann has emailed the ~~receipt~~ _________ for that Moroccan dish she served last weekend.
13. You could have put a bit less vinegar in the salad ~~sauce~~ _________. It's a bit sour.
14. What's on the ~~card~~ _________ today? – It's Friday, so it's fish!
15. A lunch ~~pause~~ _________, what's that? I never have time.
16. We stopped at this ~~guesthouse~~ _________ called *Zum weißen Lamm* and had a fantastic German meal.

E15 At work

Übersetzen Sie die deutschen Wörter und ergänzen Sie den Text.

My company has just been taken over, but most of the *(Personal)* 1. ____________ have kept their jobs. A couple of the older ones (*sind in Rente gegangen*) 2. ________________________. Business is good and a lot of us (*machen Überstunden*) 3. ____________________ on a regular basis. Our new (*Chef*) 4. ____________, or rather the new owner of the company, is an (*Unternehmer*) 5. ____________ with business interests worldwide. He only (*trifft*) 6. ____________ the big decisions and leaves the day-to-day running of his companies to local managers.

E16 Business matters

Welcher Ausdruck passt in die Lücke?

1. The ... risk on this project is great, but so too are the rewards.
   a. economic b. economical c. economous
2. Our bank account looks healthy, we are ... .
   a. in plus b. in the red c. in the black
3. The Cayman Islands is one of these off-shore ... .
   a. tax oases b. tax havens c. tax paradises
4. It's a non-profit organization. They ... any surplus they make to charity.
   a. donate b. spend c. transfer
5. Who is going to ... all the extra research?
   a. pay b. pay for c. balance
6. I don't like ... financial risks.
   a. going into b. making c. taking
7. We must prevent this happening ... .
   a. at every price b. on any price c. at all costs

1	2	3	4	5	6	7

Lösungen

A. True friends?

A1 1. c / 2. e / 3. b / 4. a / 5. d / 6. take 7. bring

▶ herbringen = bring; hin-, wegbringen = take

A2 1. brought 2. got 3. took 4. take 5. bring 6. put

▶ siehe A1

A3 1. b / 2. c / 3. d / 4. c / 5. c / 6. c / 7. d / 8. b / 9. d / 10. b

▶ herkommen = come; hinkommen = get; hingehören = go; kommen lassen = send for

A4 1. map 2. menu 3. tickets 4. card 5. ticket

▶ Landkarte = map; Speisekarte = menu; Eintritts-, Fahrkarte = ticket; Karte zum Schreiben = card

A5 1. to walk 2. last 3. go to school 4. isn't working 5. is your flight / does your plane go / does your flight go 6. run 7. That's impossible

▶ gehen (allgemein) = go; zu Fuß gehen = walk; verkehren = run, go; funktionieren = work; (an)dauern = last

A6 1. a / 2. b / 3. a / 4. b / 5. b

▶ aus dem Gedächtnis verlieren = forget; liegen lassen + Ortsbestimmung = leave

A7 1. a wine glass 2. a glass of wine 3. a jar of olives 4. a jar of honey

▶ Glas (Material, Trinkgefäß, Getränk) = glass; Glas (Aufbewahrungsgefäß mit Deckel) = jar

A8 1. salad 2. gravy 3. dressing 4. sauce 5. lettuce

▶ Salat (als Gericht/Beilage) = salad; Salat (als Pflanze/Blätter) = lettuce; Bratensoße = gravy; Salatsoße = dressing; Schokoladensoße = chocolate sauce

A9 1. sharp 2. hot/spicy

▶ scharf (Messer, Frost) = sharp; scharf (Essen) = spicy/hot

A10 1. guest 2. host 3. guest 4. customers 5. guest 6. visitor 7. passenger 8. inn 9. guesthouse

A11 1. korrekt 2. studying/revising 3. korrekt

▶ lernen (generell) = learn; für die Schule lernen, wiederholen = study/revise

A12 1. false 2. wrong 3. false 4. wrong 5. false 6. wrong 7. wrong 8. wrong 9. wrong 10. false

▶ unwahr, unecht = false; fehlerhaft, nicht korrekt = wrong

A13 1. have/take a coffee break 2. There was a short pause 3. The play was very long and there were two intervals/intermissions. 4. On some days I have so much to do that I don't take/have a lunch break. 5. Listen and repeat in the pause. 6. Break is after the second lesson.

▶ kurze Unterbrechung = pause; längere Unterbrechung, Erholungspause = break; Pause bei Konzerten o.a. = interval / intermission

A14 1. b / 2. a, b / 3. a / 4. a / 5. a / 6. a / 7. a

▶ bei Sachen mit überdurchschnittlichem Durchmesser = thick; bei Personen = fat; bei Geld o.a. (üppig) = big fat; bei Fehlern = big; bei Freunden (eng, vertraut) = close

A15 1. Does that cost extra? 2. I'll pay for the wine separately. 3. I bought the wine specially for you. 4. He did it on purpose, I'm sure.

▶ zusätzlich = extra; gesondert = separately; speziell = specially; absichtlich = on purpose

A16 1. (for) a long time 2. For twenty years 3. length 4. length 5. a long time

▶ long i.d.R. nur in Fragen und verneinten Sätzen, sonst a *long time*

A17 1. b / 2. a

▶ Preis, den man zahlt = price; Preis, den man gewinnt = prize

A18 1. Have you heard / Did you hear 2. listening 3. listened to 4. hear 5. listen 6. Listen, hear

▶ hören (akustisch wahrnehmen) = hear; hören (Radio, Musik) = listen to; zuhören, sich anhören, auf jmdn./etw. hören = listen to

A19 1. tell 2. tell 3. say 4. Say 5. tell 6. Tell

▶ angesprochene Person wird nicht genannt = say; sie wird genannt = tell. Ausnahmen: tell a story (eine Geschichte erzählen), tell the truth (die Wahrheit sagen), tell lies (lügen).

A20 1. Can you tell me what it costs / will cost? 2. I always tell the truth. 3. She said *Happy birthday,* but it wasn't my birthday. 4. She's a very quiet person. She doesn't say much. 5. What did he tell you / say to you? 6. What did he say? 7. He said he couldn't tell us anything. 8. The match was boring. – You can say that again!

▶ siehe A19

A21 1. control 2. check 3. control 4. control 5. checked 6. checked 7. checks

▶ unter Kontrolle haben, steuern = control; kontrollieren (überprüfen, ob etw. in Ordnung ist, z.B. Fahrkarten, Sicherheit) = check

A22 1. make 6. cuisine/food 7. is boiling

▶ Essen zubereiten im Allgemeinen = cook; Tee, Kaffee, Suppe zubereiten = make; sieden = boil

A23 1. warm 2. hot 3. hot 4. hot 5. hot 6. hot/warm

▶ angenehm warm = warm; unangenehm warm = hot; warm (bei Wasser, Essen) = hot

A24 1. fresh 2. chilly 3. clean 4. bright 5. Wet

A25 1. nil nil 2. zero 3. nought/zero 4. oh/zero 5. zero

▶ beim Sport = nil; bei Temperaturangaben = zero; in Dezimalzahlen = nought, zero; in Telefon- und Kontonummern = oh, zero

A26 1. latest 2. new 3. latest 4. nearest 5. Next

▶ nächste(r/s) (räumlich am nächsten) = nearest; nächste(r/s) (zeitlich/räumlich nächstfolgend) = next; neueste(r/s) (aktuellste[r/s]) = latest

A27 1. b / 2. a

▶ Motor eines kleineren Geräts = motor; Motor (bei Auto, Bus usw.) = engine

A28 1. technique 2. technology 3. technique 4. technology

▶ Methode, Arbeitsweise = technique; Wissenschaft, Technologie = technology

A29 1. shade 2. shadows 3. shadow 4. shadow 5. shade

▶ schattiger Platz = shade; Schattenumriss = shadow

A30 1. b / 2. a / 3. a / 4. a,b / 5. a / 6. a / 7. a, b / 8. b

▶ schlafen (bei Schlafgewohnheiten, -dauer, - qualität, -weise) = sleep; schlafen (im Zustand des Schlafens sein) = be asleep; ausschlafen, lange schlafen = sleep in/late

A31 1. politics 2. policy/policies 3. policy/policies

▶ Politik (politisches Leben) = politics; Politik (Handlungsweise in einem bestimmten Bereich) = policy

A32 1. They didn't have satellite TV and there were only three channels. 2. There are a lot of improvements in the new version of the program. 3. The festival programme has now appeared. 4. Which channel do you watch most?

▶ Plan = programme (GB) / program (AE); Computerprogramm = program; Fernsehkanal = channel

A33 1. office/building 2. korrekt 3. GP (= general practitioner) 4. home

▶ Wohnhaus = house; Gebäude = building; Firmenräume = office

A34 1. korrekt 2. korrekt 3. think 4. korrekt 5. think

▶ sagen wollen = mean; glauben = think

A35 1. point (0.7%) 2. comma

▶ Zeichensetzung im Text = comma; in Dezimalzahlen = point

A36 1. b / 2. b / 3. b / 4. b

▶ wollen (generell) = want; im Begriff sein, etwas zu tun = to be about to do something; nicht wollen (wenn etwas Erwünschtes nicht eintritt/eintrat) = won't/wouldn't

A37 1. Who(m) do you want to speak to/with? 2. I was just about to leave when Jim called/phoned. 3. The visitor wants to see Mr Smith. 4. I want to go to bed. 5. she just won't listen 6. I tried to open the window, but it wouldn't. 7. What are you trying to say?!

▶ siehe A36

A38 1. cost 2. costs 3. cost 4. take 5. expense 6. cost

A39 1. It's no use. 2. is good for 3. There's only one thing to do

▶ behilflich sein = help; helfen gegen (bei Arzneimitteln usw.) = be good for; nichts helfen (aussichtslos sein) = be no use/good

A40 1. richtig 2. falsch (richtig: audience)

▶ publik = public; Publikum = audience

A41 1. open air / countryside 2. human nature 3. nature

▶ natürliche Welt der Pflanzen, Tiere usw. = nature; Wesen = nature; die freie Natur = the open air / the countryside

A42 1. if 2. when 3. when 4. If 5. If 6. if 7. if 8. When 9. If

▶ unter der Bedingung, dass ... = if; bei gleichzeitig oder unmittelbar vorzeitig ablaufenden Handlungen = when

A43 1. b, c / 2. a, b / 3. b

A44 1. b / 2. a / 3. a / 4. b

▶ Tat, Handlung = action; Werbe-, Spende-, Militäraktion = campaign

A45 1. rob 2. steal 3. steal 4. rob 5. rob 6. rob 7. rob 8. steal 9. steal 10. rob

▶ einer Person/Bank etw. nehmen = rob; etw. rauben = steal

A46 1. It was cold and we had deep snow. 2. Santa Claus lives in the far north. 3. It was high summer and the grass was long. 4. How large was the amount that was stolen? 5. She has a highly paid job with a computer company. 6. The town is surrounded by high mountains. 7. Hands up! 8. The train went into the tunnel at high speed. 9. We're not expecting more than 30 people at the most. 10. More and more people are living to a great age. 11. He has heavy debts. 12. The team won by a long way / by a wide margin.

A47 1. c / 2. b, c / 3. a, b / 4. d / 5. b / 6. b / 7. Robin and Ann send their best wishes.

A48 1. street 2. road 3. road 4. street

A49 1. road 2. streets 3. street 4. roads 5. road 6. road 7. road 8. streets

A50 1. d / 2. d

▶ Stadion = stadium; in diesem Stadium = at this stage

A51 1. do 2. do 3. do 4. make 5. do 6. make 7. do 8. make 9. do 10. do 11. do 12. make

▶ herstellen, erzeugen, schaffen usw. = make; erledigen, sich beschäftigen mit = do; machen (in festen Wendungen) = have, take, go ...

A52 1. When are you having a holiday / going on holiday this year? 2. Wait, I want to take a photo. 3. It doesn't matter. 4. Shall we take/have a break? 5. I'm on a diet. 6. When are you taking your exam? 7. Don't worry.
▶ Siehe A51

A53 1. is making 2. go 3. go for 4. got 5. make 6. doing 7. make 8. do 9. have 10. done 11. doing / making
▶ Siehe A51

B. False friends

B1 1. b, c / 2. b
▶ Fabrik = factory; fabric = Stoff

B2 1. happy ending 2. korrekt 3. review
▶ Happy End = happy ending; Kritik = review; critic = Kritiker/in, Rezensent/in

B3 1. form 2. formula 3. Formula 4. formula 5. form
▶ Formular = form; formula = Formel

B4 1. b, c / 2. a, b
▶ überhören = don't hear, fail to hear; overhear = (zufällig) mithören

B5 1. branches 2. business 3. takeover 4. overtook 5. staff 6. personal 7. undertaker 8. entrepreneurs 9. boss 10. chef
▶ Branche = business; branch = Zweigstelle; Chef = boss; chef = Koch, Küchenchef; Personal = staff; personal = persönlich; Übernahme = takeover; overtake = überholen; Unternehmer = entrepreneur; undertaker = Bestattungsunternehmen

B6 1. a, b, c / 2. b
▶ Rückseite = back; backside = Hintern

B7 1. self-conscious 2. self-confident 3. sensible 4. sensitive 5. pleasant 6. sympathetic
▶ selbstbewusst = self-confident; self-conscious = gehemmt, unsicher; sensibel = sensitive; sensible = vernünftig; sympathisch = pleasant; sympathetic = mitfühlend

B8 1. a, d / 2. c
▶ ordinär = common, vulgar; ordinary = durchschnittlich, normal

B9 1. cake 2. biscuit / cookie
▶ Keks = biscuit (BE) / cookie (AE); cake = Kuchen

B10 opinion
▶ Meinung = opinion; meaning = Bedeutung

B11 1. marks/grades 2. notes 3. note 4. note 5. notice 6. notice 7. note 8. music
▶ Note = mark/grade; note = Notiz, Zettel; Notiz = note; notice = Anschlag

B12 1. d / 2. c
▶ bekommen = get/have/receive; become = werden

B13 1. When is the courier going to pick up / collect the parcels? 2. ... a package of measures 3. I use several Microsoft software packages. 4. Two packets of butter and a packet of tea.
▶ Paket = parcel, package; packet = Päckchen

B14 1. korrekt 2. draft 3. plan 4. threw him
▶ Konzept = plan/draft; concept = Begriff

B15 1. a map 2. a tablet 3. a folder 4. a tray 5. a photograph 6. a photographer
▶ Mappe = folder; map = Landkarte; Tablett = tray; tablet = Tablette; Fotograf = photographer; photograph = Foto

B16 1. murder 2. murderer 3. poison 4. gifts
▶ Mörder = murderer; murder = Mord; Gift = poison; gift = Geschenk

B17 1. I paid and the taxi driver gave me a receipt. 2. It tastes wonderful. You must give me the recipe. 3. The prescription still has to be signed by the doctor. 4. What's your recipe for success?
▶ Rezept (beim Arzt) = prescription; Rezept (beim Kochen oder als Erfolgsrezept) = recipe; receipt = Quittung

B18 1. b / 2. b, c / 3. c
▶ Rente = pension; rent = Miete

B19 1. valid, up to date 2. topical 3. current
▶ gültig = valid; von momentanem Interesse = topical; gegenwärtig = current; actual(ly) = tatsächlich

B20 1. spare 2. save 3. spent 4. donate 5. save
▶ sparen = save; spare = entbehren; spenden = donate; spend = (Geld) ausgeben; (Zeit) verbringen

B21 1. mobile (phone) / cell phone 2. indicated 3. overlooked
▶ übersehen = overlook; oversee = beaufsichtigen; Handy = mobile (phone) (BE) / cell phone (AE); handy = praktisch, griffbereit; blinken = indicate; blink = zwinkern

B22 1. c / 2. a / 3. b, d
▶ Gymnasium = grammar school; gymnasium = Turn-, Sporthalle; Mobbing = bullying; mob = belagern; brav = good; brave = mutig;

B23 1. Gymnastics 2. exercises 3. wandering 4. hiking
▶ Gymnastik (Wettkampfdisziplin) = gymnastics; Gymnastik (private Freiübungen) = exercises; wandern = hike; wander = ziellos streifen, bummeln

B24 1. brochures 2. advertisement 3. prospects 4. announcements
▶ Prospekt = brochure; prospect = Aussicht; Annonce = advertisement; announcement = Bekanntgabe, Ankündigung

B25 1. founded 2. founded 3. grounded
▶ gründen = found; ground = Startverbot erhalten (bei Flugzeugen)

B26 1. at last, finally 2. sometime, one day

▶ eventually = schließlich, endlich

B27 1. a, b, c / 2. b, c, d

▶ eventuell = may ..., ... possibly ..., (it's) possible ...

B28 1. material/fabric 2. material / fabric 3. substances 4. material

▶ Stoff (Gewebe) = material/fabric; Stoff (natürlicher Bestandteil) = substance; Stoff (Handlung) = material; stuff = Zeug

B29 1. d / 2. a

▶ Warenhaus = department store; warehouse = Lager(haus)

B30 1. denomination 2. confession

▶ Konfession = denomination; confession = Beichte

B31 1. engaged 2. dedicated 3. committed 4. involved 5. active 6. hired

▶ engagiert = involved, dedicated, committed; engaged = verlobt

C. Lots of friends

C1 1. husband 2. man 3. woman 4. wife 5. My goodness / Oh boy!

▶ Frau / Mann (weiblicher / männlicher Mensch) = man / woman; Ehefrau / -mann = wife / husband

C2 1. b / 2. c / 3. a / 4. e / 5. d

▶ in Bitten, Fragen = please; Reaktion auf Dank = not at all / that's OK / it's a pleasure ...; Reaktion auf Entschuldigung = it's/that's all right / never mind; Zustimmung zu einer Bitte = certainly / of course / please do; wie bitte? = sorry? excuse me? pardon?; beim Überreichen = here you are.

C3 1. Certainly. / Of course. / Please do. 2. Here you are. 3. Sorry? / Pardon? / Excuse me? 4. please 5. It's a pleasure. / That's all right. / You're welcome.

▶ siehe C2

C4 1. When 2. than 3. as 4. As

▶ zeitlich = when; bei Komparativen = than; „genau wie" = as; als (ob) = as (if); in der Eigenschaft als ... = as

C5 1. visit 2. attend / go to 3. go to

▶ besuchen (als Gast, Tourist usw.) = visit; besuchen (Schule, Kirche usw.) = attend/go to; besuchen (kulturelle Veranstaltungen) = go to

C6 1. pay 2. pay for 3. pay 4. pay for 5. pay 6. pay 7. pay for 8. pay 9. pay 10. pay for

▶ bei Produkten und Dienstleistungen = pay for; bei Personen, Beträgen, Rechnungen = pay

C7 1. memory 2. remember 3. memories 4. short-term memory 5. remember 6. remind 7. reminder 8. remembers

▶ sich erinnern = remember; jmdn. erinnern = remind somebody; Erinnerung (im Gedächtnis) = memory; Erinnerung (Gedächtnisstütze) = reminder; Gedächtnis = memory

C8 Across: 3. fit 5. well 6. good for you
Down: 1. better 2. healthy 4. common

▶ in guter körperlicher Verfassung = healthy / fit; genesen = better; gesundheitsfördernd = good for you

C9 1. b / 2. c / 3. c / 4. c / 5. a / 6. b / 7. b / 8. a. / 9. b / 10. b / 11. a

▶ fahren (ganz allgemein) = go; bei Auto = drive; bei Fahrrad und Motorrad = ride; mit Geschwindigkeitsangabe = do / travel at; im Sinne von „verkehren" = run; fahren mit Verkehrsmitteln = take

C10 1. instructor 2. teacher 3. instructor 4. instructor 5. teacher 6. instructors 7. teachers

▶ Lehrer für Kopfarbeit = teacher; Lehrer für praktische Fertigkeiten = instructor

C11 1. tight 2. close 3. narrow 4. closely

▶ schmal = narrow; eng anliegend, stramm = tight; nahe, vertraut = close; als Adverb = closely

C12 1. about 2. for 3. around/about 4. to 5. to 6. into 7. for

▶ etw. dagegen tun = do something about; als Schutz gegen etw. = for; zeitlich = around / about; bei Widerstand o.a. = to; bei Austausch = for

C13 1. a / 2. a / 3. a / 4. b / 5. b

▶ als Schauspieler auftreten = act; aufführen = perform; sich abspielen = to be set; (eine Rolle) spielen = play

C14 1. tall 2. big/great 3. great 4. big/great 5. large 6. big 7. great 8. big 9. great 10. big/large 11. big/great 12. great

▶ bei Sachen = big; bei Menschen = tall; im Sinne von kräftig, älter = big; beträchlich = big, great (bei Nomen ohne Plural nur great möglich); berühmt, bedeutend = great; umsatzstark, erfolgreich = big; bei Mengen, Dimensionen = large

C15 1. smaller 2. little 3. little 4. small 5. small 6. small 7. small 8. small 9. little 10. little

▶ als neutraler Ausdruck = small; emotional gefärbt (niedlich / schrecklich klein) = little; jünger = little

C16 1. hear 2. understand 3. hear

▶ begreifen = understand; akustisch wahrnehmen = hear

C17 Across: 1. stay 3. remains 4. stopped
Down: 1. standing 2. keep

▶ im gleichen Zustand bleiben = stay, keep; am gleichen Ort bleiben = stay; übrig bleiben = remain; stehenbleiben (nicht mehr gehen) = stop

C18 1. fast 2. quick 3. fast 4. quick 5. fast 6. quickly

▶ schnell (von der Bewegung her) = fast; schnell (nur kurze Zeit beanspruchend) = quick

C19 1. room 2. square 3. is this seat taken 4. courts 5. course 6. sports ground 7. place 8. have a seat 9. place 10. room

▶ Ort, Stelle, Studienplatz = place; ausreichend Raum = room, space; in einer Stadt = square; beim Tennis = court; beim Golf = course; Sitzplatz = seat

C20 1. drive / journey / trip 2. weekend trip 3. ten-minute bus ride 4. travel 5. tour 6. car journeys

▶ Reise generell (meist Vergnügungsreise mit Aufenthalt am Zielort) = trip; als Autofahrt = drive; längere Fahrt ohne Aufenthalt = journey; das Reisen = travel; Rundreise = tour

C21 1. How long does it take from here to Strasbourg? 2. It takes about four hours by car. 3. It took me two whole days to get my presentation ready. 4. I know. That sort of thing takes a lot of time.

▶ brauchen (Zeit) = take

C22 1. I need your help. It will only take a few minutes. 2. You don't need to / You needn't wait for me. 3. By train it takes one and a half hours. 4. The journey takes one and a half hours. 5. The film lasts 30 minutes. 6. You don't need to / You needn't bring anything with you, we have everything. 7. I need another two hours. This sort of job/work takes a long time.

▶ etw./jmdn. benötigen = need; brauchen nicht zu … = don't need to / needn't; brauchen (Zeit) = take/last

C23 1. b / 2. b / 3. b / 4. a / 5. b / 6. b / 7. b / 8. a / 9. a / 10. b / 11. b / 12. b / 13. a, b / 14. b / 15. b / 16. a

▶ mit Hand / Körperteil halten = hold; in einem Zustand belassen = keep; jmdn. festhalten = stop; bei Versprechen = keep; bei Rede = make, give; jmdn. für etw. ansehen = think of someone as something; sich halten an = stick to; (an)dauern = last

C24 1. suit 2. suit 3. fit 4. fit 5. match

▶ passen (Größe, Dimensionen) = fit; gut stehen = suit; passen (zu etw. anderem) = match; recht sein = suit

C25 1. a, c / 2. d / 3. a, c, d / 4. c / 5. a, b / 6. d

▶ studieren = be a student, be at / go to university; Studium = subject, (university/degree) course

C26 1. with 2. at 3. With 4. near 5. for/with 6. at/on 7. over 8. at 9. in 10. on/with 11. at 12. at 13. with

▶ bei jdm zu Hause = with someone / at someone's house; in der Nähe von = near; bei Firma = for; bei Bedingungen = at

C27 1. job 2. work 3. work 4. job 5. job 6. job

▶ Arbeit (allgemein oder als Arbeitsort) = work; einzelne, bestimmte Arbeit, Anstellung = job
Beachten Sie: work kann nicht mit dem unbestimmten Artikel stehen.

C28 1. recognized 2. realized/recognized 3. realized 4. realized 5. recognized

▶ mit den Sinnen wiedererkennen = recognize; geistig entdecken = realize; politisch = recognize

C29 Across: 1. eventually 3. finally 4. after all
Down: 1. end 2. at last

▶ als Folge, am Schluss = eventually, in the end; später als erwartet bzw. gewünscht = finally; schließlich doch, wenn man es richtig betrachtet = after all; endlich nach langem Ersehnen = at last

C30 1. light 2. slight 3. easy 4. a slight 5. A light 6. I found it easy

▶ einfach = easy; geringfügig = slight; von geringem Gewicht = light

C31 1. by 2. of 3. out of 4. of mine 5. by 6. of

▶ bei Urhebern = by

C32 1. c / 2. a, c / 3. b, c / 4. a / 5. c / 6. c / 7. b, c / 8. a / 9. c / 10. b, c / 11. b / 12. b, c

▶ schwer (von Gewicht) = heavy; schwierig = difficult, hard; ernsthaft = serious

C33 1. b / 2. c / 3. a / 4. c

C34 1. bad 2. poor 3. off 4. sick 5. poorly

▶ negativ = bad; sich schlecht (krank) fühlen = feel sick; bei Qualität = poor; bei Lebensmitteln = off

C35 1. Everybody / Everyone thinks the same. 2. I'm prepared/willing to do anything to help you. 3. Every two or three days I get an email. 4. My motto is: All or nothing. 5. We all need a break. 6. Everybody / Everyone was enthusiastic.

C36 1. a / 2. b / 3. a / 4. b / 5. a / 6. a / 7. b / 8. b / 9. b / 10. b

▶ bis (+ zeitlicher Endpunkt) = till/until; bis spätestens = by; bei Mengen-/Zahlenangaben = up to; räumlich = as far as / to

C37 1. the same age 2. the same size 3. the same clothes

▶ gleich + bestimmtes Adjektiv = the same + Nomen

C38 1. Have you finished? 2. Are you ready for dessert?

▶ bereit = ready; erledigt, abgeschossen = finished

C39 1. c, speak 2. a, at 3. e, do 4. b, get on 5. f, could 6. d, go/carry

C40 1. be / become 2. go 3. are turning 4. is becoming / is getting 5. grow 6. has turned out 7. got 8. is going

▶ Berufspläne = be / become; Zustandsveränderung = get / become; Negativveränderung = go; allmähliche Veränderung = grow; Farbveränderung = turn / go

C41 1. realize 2. note 3. noticed

▶ sich geistig bewusst werden = realize; mit den Sinnen wahrnehmen = notice; sich merken = note, remember

C42 1. recently/lately 2. At the beginning 3. in the next (few) weeks/months

C43 1. Have you ever been to Mexico? 2. I've been to New York before. 3. I would like to visit Ireland sometime. 4. Listen carefully because I'm only going to say it once. 5. Once upon a time there was a king 6. The town was once famous.

C44 1. ex-husband 2. a previous marriage 3. used to live 4. sooner 5. once 6. previous 7. former 8. a previous 9. once 10. used to meet

▶ vorhergehend = previous; ehemalig = former / ex; früher (eher) = earlier/sooner; früher einmal = once; früher habe/bin ich immer ... = I used to ...

C45 1. he's having 2. it says 3. suits 4. stand 5. is complete/finished

C46 1. b / 2. b / 3. a / 4. b

▶ während (Konjunktion) = while; während (Präposition vor Nomen) = during

C47 1. strong 2. heavy 3. heavily 4. hard 5. great 6. heavy 7. badly 8. strong 9. heavily 10. 600-page long

▶ bei Regen, Rauchen, Verkehr = heavy

C48 Across: 4. outside 5. in front of
Down: 1. ago 2. with 3. before 6. to

▶ räumlich = in front of/outside; zeitlich (Gegenteil von „nach") = before; zeitlich (im Sinne von „her") = ago; bei Uhrzeit = to

C49 1. quiet 2. calm 3. calm 4. quiet 5. still

▶ leise, unauffällig, schweigsam = quiet; ruhig, gelassen, reglos = calm / still (Sitzen)

C50 1. How are things? Everything OK? 2. What was the weather like? 3. What's the new boss like? 4. How do you say that in English? 5. What's this thing called in English? 6. What's the phone number? 7. What was it like travelling alone? 8. It's a building like a hotel. 9. He's not as old as her. 10. We trusted him, as many people did.

C51 1. even 2. Me too 3. So do I 4. Neither will we 5. either 6. Even if 7. so

C52 1. aware / conscious 2. aware 3. consciously 4. conscious 5. conscious

▶ um etw. wissend = aware / conscious (bei „as far as ..." nur aware möglich, vor Nomen nur conscious möglich); wissentlich = conscious(ly); ...-bewusst = ...-conscious

C53 1. The police wanted to see my driving licence (BE) / driver's license (AE). 2. Our son has just started taking driving lessons. 3. Our daughter has already passed her (driving) test. / Our daughter already has a driving licence / driver's license.

C54 1. wear 2. carry 3. supported 4. carry 5. bear 6. bears 7. wear 8. bear 9. wear

▶ befördern = carry; am Körper anhaben = wear; im übertragenen Sinne = bear

C55 1. a / 2. a / 3. a / 4. c / 5. a / 6. a, b / 7. c / 8. b / 9. a / 10. b / 11. a / 12. a, b, c / 13. b, c / 14. b / 15. b

▶ räumlich = above/over; betreffend = about; auf dem Wege = via; bei Zahlenangaben = over

C56 1. nein 2. ja 3. nein 4. ja 5. ja 6. nein 7. ja 8. ja 9. nein 10. ja

2. It's already half past two. 4. Has Tony phoned yet? 5. Even before he got/stood up, I knew what he would say. 7. Have you ever been to Disneyland? / Have you been to Disneyland before? 8. The first guests are already here / have already arrived. 10. Very soon we shall/will hear the first results.

D. Confusing friends

D1 1. advice 2. advise

▶ advice = Rat(schlag) (Nomen); advise = (be)raten (Verb)

D2 1. b / 2. a

▶ homework = Hausaufgabe(n); housework = Haushaltsarbeit(en)

D3 1. a / 2. b / 3. a

▶ interesting = interessant; interested = interessiert

D4 1. Is the Sahara the largest desert in the world? 2. What would you like for dessert?

▶ desert = Wüste; dessert = Dessert

D5 1. economic 2. economic 3. economical 4. economic 5. economical 6. economical

▶ economic = die Wirtschaft betreffend; economical = sparsam

D6 1. classical 2. korrekt 3. classical 4. korrekt 5. korrekt 6. classical

▶ classic = angesehen, typisch, von bleibendem Wert; classical = klassisch (in Bezug auf Musik, die Antike)

D7 1. beside 2. besides 3. besides 4. besides 5. Besides working 6. beside

▶ beside = (örtlich) neben; besides = neben (= außer), außerdem

D8 1. It's 2. its 3. its 4. its 5. It's 6. its

▶ it's = es ist (= it is); its = sein, ihr

D9 1. altogether 2. all together

▶ altogether = insgesamt; all together = alle zusammen

D10 1. lie 2. lays 3. lain 4. lied 5. lying 6. laid 7. lying 8. lay 9. laid, laid 10. lay, lain 11. lied, lied

D11 1. largely 2. largely 3. greatly 4. greatly

▶ largely = größtenteils; greatly = sehr

D12 1. passed 2. past 3. passed 4. past 5. past 6. past 7. past 8. passed

▶ passed = Form des Verbs pass (vergehen, überholen, vorbeigehen an); past = Präposition / Adverb (an ... vorbei, vorbei)

D13 1. a / 2. b

▶ terrible = furchtbar; terrific = gewaltig, toll

D14 1. used to work 2. had to get used to writing 3. get used to it 4. am used to using

▶ used to (+ Verb in Grundform) = früher + Verb in der Vergangenheit; be used to (+ -ing-Form) = es gewohnt sein, zu ...; get used to = sich gewöhnen an

D15 1. at last 2. at least

D16 1. risen 2. raised 3. raised 4. rose 5. rose 6. raise

▶ raise, raised, raised = an-, auf-, hochheben; rise, rose, risen = steigen, an-, auf-, hochsteigen, sich erheben

D17 1. a / 2. b

▶ sometime = irgendwann; sometimes = manchmal

D18 1. a / 2. b

▶ every day = jeden Tag; everyday = alltäglich

D19 1. historic 2. historical 3. historical 4. historical

▶ historic = historisch (= bedeutsam); historical = geschichtlich, aus der Geschichte

D20 1. b / 2. a

▶ affect = beeinflussen, betreffen (Verb); effect = Auswirkung (Nomen)

D21 1. loose 2. lose 3. lose 4. loose

▶ loose = lose; lose = verlieren

D22 1. mayor 2. major

▶ major = Major; mayor = Bürgermeister

D23 1. b / 2. b / 3. a

▶ in time = rechtzeitig; on time = pünktlich

E. All friends together

E1 1. I'll have 2. menu 3. cuisine / food 4. mobile (phone) (BE) / cell phone (AE) 5. inn/pub 6. opinion

E2 1. play/piece 2. audience 3. interval 4. poorly attended

E3 1. commercial 2. channels 3. newsreaders 4. latest

E4 1. a / 2. b / 3. b / 4. b / 5. a / 6. a

E5 1. trays 2. menu 3. salad bar 4. good for you 5. salad dressing

E6 1. answer it 2. code 3. take the call 4. ask for 5. dial 6. hung up

E7 1. reunion 2. grammar school 3. at 4. marks/grades 5. did/took 6. bullied 7. took/passed 8. went to/started university

E8 1. did / went on 2. stay 3. guesthouses 4. hot 5. took 6. It took us 7. checked 8. forms 9. Altogether

E9 1. sleep in 2. ride 3. used to drive 4. two years ago 5. took 6. hard 7. road 8. the open air 9. hiking 10. photographer 11. am also interested in 12. classic 13. are set in

E10 1. lately/recently 2. three months 3. latest 4. At this stage 5. current 6. during/over 7. take 8. does it take 9. than

E11 1. I like Ronaldo's wife a lot. / Ronaldo's wife is very nice. 2. Anna is very self-confident. 3. Mark is my son from my/a previous marriage. 4. I'm the same age as my boss. 5. Be careful. He's very sensitive. 6. Please leave me alone / in peace. I have to (do some) work. 7. My riding instructor is very tall, almost/nearly two metres tall. 8. Be sensible! 9. Why are you so quiet today? 10. When was the last time we were all together? 11. My husband is one of the few men who are not interested in football. 12. The children were very good.

E12 1. Surgery hours 2. good for you 3. prescription 4. painkillers 5. false teeth 6. a really bad sore throath

E13 1. next 2. nearest 3. shade 4. shadow 5. backside 6. back

E14 1. lettuce 2. boiled potatoes 3. hot/spicy 4. drinking water 5. tray 6. Bon appétit / Enjoy it 7. makes me/you fat 8. have a barbecue 9. hot 10. leftovers 11. loaf 12. recipe 13. dressing 14. menu 15. break 16. inn

E15 1. staff 2. have gone into retirement / have retired 3. do / are doing overtime 4. boss 5. entrepreneur 6. takes/makes

E16 1. a / 2. c / 3. b / 4. a / 5. b / 6. c / 7. c

TELL ME MORE® Version 9.0
TV-Nachrichten Englisch
Je 1 DVD-ROM
Installationsblatt
Headset
ISBN 978–3–19–809576–8

Für Profis und alle, die es werden wollen!

TELL ME MORE® Version 9.0 TV-Nachrichten Englisch macht für Sie das Englischlernen zu einem Erlebnis! Das Programm eignet sich bestens als Ergänzungsmaterial, um das Hör- und Sprachverständnis zu verbessern. Die Themenschwerpunkte reichen von Politik und Wirtschaft über Kultur und Gesellschaft bis hin zu Umwelt und Technologie.

- Ca. 50 Lektionen auf der Basis hockaktueller euronews®-Videos
- Interaktiver Übungsapparat mit Wortfeldübungen, Lückentexten u.v.m.
- Lernfortschritts- und Zertifikatstest
- Für die englische Ausgabe: kostenlose wöchentliche Online-Lektion basierend auf aktuellen euronews®-Videos
- Freie Wahl der Ausgangssprache (Deutsch, Englisch, Französisch, Italienisch und Spanisch)

Auch für Französisch und Spanisch verfügbar.

www.hueber.de

Hueber Freude an Sprach